Growing the World's
Largest Church

Karen Hurston

CHRISM

Springfield, Missouri

02-0329

Chrism books are published by Gospel Publishing House.

2nd Printing 1995

Library of Congress Cataloging-in-Publication Data

Hurston, Karen.
    Growing the world's largest church / Karen Hurston.
        p.   cm.
    Includes bibliographical references.
    ISBN 0-88243-329-6
      1. Cho, Yong-gi, 1936– 2. Yŏŭido Sun Pogŭm Kyohoe (Seoul, Korea) 3. Pentecostal churches—Korea (South)—History—20th century. 4. Korea—Church history—20th century. 5. Church growth—Korea (South)   I. Title.
BR164.5.K6H87   1994
289.9′4′ 095195—dc20   94-18796

To John and Maxine Hurston,
my mentors, my models of excellence in ministry,
my hero and heroine of the faith, my best friends.
I continually thank God you are my parents.

Table of Contents

Foreword \ 7
Acknowledgments \ 9
Introduction \ 11

1. The Early Years \ 19
2. The Ministry of Prayer \ 36
3. International Prayer Mountain \ 50
4. The Ministry of Layleaders \ 62
5. Home Cell Groups \ 81
6. The Ministry of the Pastoral Staff \ 108
7. Outreach Followships \ 124
8. The Church's Doctrine \ 135
9. The Sermons \ 147
10. The Worship Services \ 160

Small Group Discussion \ 181

Appendix 1: The Later Years \ 191
Appendix 2: Deacons in One Church
   in America \ 197
Appendix 3: Three Kinds of Group Systems \ 199
Appendix 4: Home Visitation in Church
   History \ 207
Endnotes \ 211

Foreword

I first met Karen Hurston when she was seven years old. I remember the times that she and her mother, Maxine, would come to the tent church and sit cross-legged on straw mats as I preached.

Later, I and her father, John, an Assemblies of God missionary who served with me over a span of twenty years, baptized Karen in the waters of the Han River. Then, after we had made the transition to Sodaemoon in the prefabricated building John had brought from America, Karen received what we term the baptism in the Holy Spirit during a worship service. Karen was also the young girl present in the emergency room of the hospital after I had a nervous collapse. It was after that point that God began to speak to me about the "church in the home," which later became the home cell system so prevalent throughout our church today.

In 1976, an adult Karen came to serve on my staff for five years and, with her father, started Church Growth International. In those five years we held more than a hundred seminars, touching the lives of forty thousand church leaders.

Since 1985 Karen has been serving in many churches around the world as a speaker and consultant, particularly in the area of cell groups and home visitation. During that time she has made numerous trips back to Korea to do further study of our church.

This book represents research that has been collected over a fourteen-year period. Karen has held countless interviews, conducted surveys, and asked many probing questions.

In this book, Karen has communicated much of what I have known to be at the heart of our church and congregational life. I highly commend its reading to you.

—DR. YONGGI CHO
Pastor
Yoido Full Gospel Church
Seoul, Korea

Acknowledgments

Many have contributed much to make this book a reality. First, Dr. Yonggi Cho, thank you for permission to research your great church. To those who work closely with Dr. Cho—Rev. Lydia Swain, Rev. Haegyu Lee, Ms. Minsook Lee, and Mrs. Ruth Sholtis—you all were great help and encouragement through this process. May God bless you richly for your diligent work for his Kingdom. To the many who helped me with interpretation and translation—my special friend Lee Weeder, Miran Kwan, Rev. Dongwhan Yim, Senior Deacon Dongho Kim, and others whose names are buried in a sea of notes—I give heartfelt thanks and appreciation.

Rev. Kisuk Hong, Rev. Songjin Bin, Rev. Leebu Pak, and my many past and present YFGC pastoral staff friends, I can never thank you enough for your patience as I accompanied you in visitation and asked what seemed to be an unending number of questions. Rev. Yongchan Cho, thank you for your help and encouragement; you indeed are a good *Oppa* (Korean for "older brother"). To YFGC's outstanding section and cell leaders— including Yunghu Yu, Taeho Kim, Okja Kim, Gabsun Cha, Guisoon Chang, Dongwha Lee, Kyungshin Park, Heechong Lee, Daegyu Park, and Jungoon Chea—I celebrate all the wonderful things God is doing in your lives. To the outstanding YFGC layelders who have been a great help to me—Duchun Cho, Chulik Lee, Kyungshin Park, Hangki Kim, Soontae Kim, Sokho

Kim, Kangman Lee, Chanho Chong, with special regards to Changki Song.*

To the many pastors who had me consult and speak at your churches, I give special thanks to Steve Allen, Tommy Barnett, Frank Bailey, Harold Caballeros, Sam Carr, Bill Gardner, Bruce Klepp, Fred Rodriguez, Larry Stockstill, David Sumrall, Jim and Jean Thompson, and Roland Wells. To my friends and partners in prayer—Gwen Aldridge, Jody Boudreaux, Lucinda Dise, Rebecca Fuentes, Agnes Hall, Diane Hartman, Daniel Haupt, Angie Rhodes, Lee Weeder, and Vicki Wilson—no expression of gratitude would ever be adequate.

David Womack, Glen Ellard, Jean Lawson, and others at Gospel Publishing House, thank you for the many hours you have spent editing and working on this book. Pam Campbell and Jan Rogers, thank you for your suggestions in the earlier versions.

Dad and Mom, how can I ever repay you for all your help and insights, your many readings of present and former manuscripts, your needed prayer, unbelievable patience, and continuing encouragement? Without you, both this book and I would not exist.

And, Lord, most of all, I thank You. You are the Potter who shaped a piece of clay in Seoul, Korea, to later tell part of this story: How You used ordinary people to do extraordinary things when they kept their eyes turned in Your direction!

*Please note that there is a variation in the English spelling of the phonetic pronunciation of Korean names. Also, since Dr. Cho chose to combine his first and second given Korean names into one—Yonggi—I have opted to do the same with other Korean names. Moreover, while married Korean women keep their maiden family names, you will often see that I have called them "Mrs. (Husband's family name)" in order to keep a constancy for our western framework.

Introduction

I was only seven years old when I first met Grace, the young woman who would become Dr. Yonggi Cho's wife. She was a fun-loving, diligent high school student, as well as a gifted pianist. One of the first times we talked, our families were enjoying a day of leisure together. I remember how Grace sat on the edge of the hotel pool, her legs dangling in the water. And I noticed how often Dr. Cho, pastor of a church housed in a tent, glanced in her direction as he talked with her mother, Jashil Choi.

Now, more than thirty years later, Grace sat across from me again. During those years, she had married Yonggi Cho, given birth to three sons, earned her doctorate in piano, and become a grandmother. Her dark eyes gleamed as we laughed and talked of earlier times and of answers to prayer. She was a caring person, pleasant to be around.

Then our conversation drifted to Yoido (yo-EE-doe) Full Gospel Church (YFGC). I spoke of the church's cell groups, layleaders, and outreach fellowships. "Some people wonder why this church has grown so large," she said. "Our relationship with God is like a two-way street. What we receive from God, we are to minister to one another."

She explained, "Once you receive the baptism in the Holy Spirit, you naturally want to minister to others. As you freely minister to others what God has already ministered to you, God gives you even more grace and blessing. When you are faithful to care for and minister to and pray with others out of that increase of grace and blessing, God responds by giving you even more. In this way, revival never has to stop; it just grows. This is what the church and cell groups are all about. The Christian who does not do this is unhappy and unfruitful."

A Vision for Growth

It was in 1979 that YFGC, a church in Seoul, Korea, announced that it had passed the 100,000-member mark—the largest single congregation in church history—and the Christian world took note. Religious magazines carried the amazing account of its pastor, Dr. Yonggi Cho. Yet, the growth did not end there, for within two years the congregation had doubled!

Some scoffed when Dr. Cho stated that God had given him a vision for half a million members, but in 1985 they stopped laughing as membership climbed past that mark. By January 1992, thirty-four years after the church began, the membership had reached 645,296, even after church leaders had encouraged 50,000 members to leave the congregation for the creation of two new congregations.

Church growth and revival are not foreign to South Korea. According to church growth researcher Dr. John Vaughan, twenty-four of the world's fifty largest churches are in South Korea.[1] But no church, not even on Korean soil, has come close to the vast membership of YFGC.

How did such remarkable growth come about? What are the Christians of this church doing that others are not?

YFGC is more than a remarkable example of growth to me; it is the church in which I grew up. My parents, missionaries John and Maxine Hurston, began working with Dr. Cho in 1960, when church facilities were just a dilapidated tent in a destitute part of town. I remember seeing more and more people, mostly poor, sick, and struggling, come to that tent to hear about Jesus Christ. They learned that He died for their sins, could heal their broken bodies, and could help them prosper in this life as well as the next.

I also remember when the church moved to a new structure in a more central area of Seoul. Shortly after that, in 1962, Dad and Dr. Cho baptized me in the gently flowing waters of Seoul's Han River. As I walked from the river in a white dripping dress that day to join hundreds of others on a grassy hill, I knew I was part of something larger than myself. But none of us knew how much greater this move of God in Seoul would become.

Fifteen years later, I began five years as a staff member of YFGC. Once again I observed firsthand the increase and struggles of this church's ministry as it grew from forty thousand to two-hundred thousand members.

Discovering Principles of Growth

Starting in the late 1970s, hundreds of pastors from around the world traveled to Korea to try to discover YFGC's secret for growth. I'll never forget one of those American pastors. He observed the twelve weekly services—seven on Sunday, three on Wednesday, and two on Saturday—where thirty-five thousand people packed into the massive sanctuary and latecomers watched closed-circuit video in a series of auxiliary chapels. The American pastor was awed by the hundreds of children's Sunday school classes, the eleven regional sanctuaries in outlying areas around Seoul, the variety of "mission fellowships," and the masses of believers who scattered to do volunteer work on Sunday afternoons.

During the week, that same American pastor accompanied a staff pastor and a lay section leader as they visited homes, a pattern they follow five days a week. On Wednesday, he journeyed to one of the four daily services held at Prayer Mountain, YFGC's prayer retreat where more than one million people come each year. Friday evening he joined a men's home cell group—one of thirty thousand such gatherings—then attended two hours of the Friday all-night prayer meeting and learned that thousands pray all night, six nights a week.

Before returning to America, that minister said, "I had heard Dr. Cho speak in the United States and decided to come and see the world's largest church for myself. I feel like the Queen of Sheba after she had seen Solomon's kingdom: 'Not even half was told me' [1 Kings 10:6–7]."

What is that half that hasn't been told? What can we learn from this church? Has this church developed a spiritual dynamic that can be applied for lasting growth anywhere in the world?

Cultural Differences

Before we examine the principles and practices that led to the growth of the world's largest church, consider two major misconceptions many have had about YFGC. The first is that some consider Korea to be such a different culture that any church or religious movement in that country could not possibly be applicable to America.

In pondering this often-voiced protest, I remembered how Paul referred to Jesus as a "stumbling stone" (see Romans 9:32–33). Jesus did not fulfill the Jews' expectations of a military Messiah who would overthrow the Roman government and establish an earthly rule, and as a result, many stumbled over Him and rejected the truth He offered.

For some, perhaps the example of YFGC is a stumbling stone to the truths God would emphasize through it as the world's largest church. As with any stumbling stone, we each have a choice: We can dismiss the importance of YFGC, or we can listen and learn the truths God would relay through its example.

Consider five parallels between YFGC and America. First, Dr. Cho began this church in a city in ruins after three years of war.[2] In America's most prominent cities, mounting racial tensions have erupted into riots and violence. Nationwide in 1990, there were a reported two million violent crimes of murder, rape, robbery, or aggravated assault.[3] American cities face immense difficulties, lying in the ruins of racism, crime, and drug abuse—visible signs of a deteriorating quality of life. Like the postwar Koreans, we Americans also need the restoration only Jesus Christ through His church can offer.

Second, YFGC started in the midst of broken families and societal upheaval following the Korean War. Similarly, many American families now battle the war of divorce, while television programs build on the tragic comedy of single parents and blended families. Children are often unwilling targets in this devastation, with the most typical abuse victim being a white seven-year-old female.[4] These wounded American families also need the gospel of Jesus, which mends families and heals the brokenhearted.

Third, even from the beginning Dr. Cho preached to the poor the startling message that God would make their lives better, here and now in this life. We, too, are surrounded by the poor, with one in seven Americans living below the poverty level.[5] Every night in major metropolitan areas thousands of displaced children, elderly, and jobless sleep in emergency shelters, welfare hotels, and abandoned buildings and cars. Countless more live on the edge financially: They're the faces you see at the hotel carrying your bags, the people selling newspapers on the corner, the ones behind the counter at fast-food restaurants and at service stations—people earning a minimum wage. The struggling and homeless in America also need the hope only Jesus can give.

Fourth, Dr. Cho's challenge was to mobilize laypeople who were already working long hours and coping with urban pressures. Korean men are reputed to work more hours than anyone else in the industrialized world, typically ten hours a day, five and one-half days a week. Our challenge is much the same. Stress in American work and family life has resulted in heart disease being the leading cause of death, whether one is a white-collar executive or a blue-collar factory worker.[6]

Fifth, YFGC began and flourished in the midst of Eastern religions and animism—which include many expressions of the occult. In America, the alarming rise of satanism and witchcraft is found in the dark side of the New Age revival of the occult. Thoroughgoing New Age stores position Shirley MacLaine's latest best-seller next to the satanic rituals of Alcister Crowley and books like *Witchcraft and the Gay Counterculture*.[7] American-style pagan spirituality has created a confused void that only new birth in Jesus Christ can genuinely fill.

Elements of Growth

In addition to the misconception that cultural differences between Korea and America would prevent the application of church growth principles is the misconception that just one or two elements resulted in the growth of YFGC.

The responses of most visitors to YFGC remind me of the familiar story of the blind men who journeyed to discover what an elephant was like. One felt the elephant's tail and decided an elephant is like a rope. Another felt the elephant's leg and decided an elephant is like a tree. Another felt his ear, deciding an elephant is like a fan, and so on. Each man was correct from his perspective, but no one man had the full picture.

My father, John Hurston, says: "Many have come to observe YFGC and have left with a partial understanding of one or two of its aspects—usually its dynamic prayer life and home cell groups. But other key factors are often overlooked. The common thread throughout is the people's strong commitment to partner with God and with one another in ministry. To focus on just one aspect is to miss the total picture."

I am writing this book to share the total picture, to show each major factor contributing to this great church. I have made three recent research trips[8] to Seoul because I have wanted other Christians to know the half that has yet to be told. And still the picture will not be complete, at least not statistically. As with any growing entity, one must expect change. Accordingly, the figures of YFGC do not remain static, for people continue to find their place there. So the statistics throughout this book are current to the time of this printing.

This book will examine the crucial spiritual dynamics of YFGC, including the distinctiveness of the congregation's prayer life, the sermons and church services, the laystructure, and the pastoral team.

Dr. Yonggi Cho has already written several books in English about certain aspects of his church. However, I write as an American who grew up in his church and my view is taken from that of the congregation. Perhaps God has something to say to all of us in the way He has shaped the world's largest church.

At times we think that incredible things happened only in the first-century church or that if they can happen today, then only somewhere far away on the "mission field." But all around are lost and hurting people—unbelievers eternally lost without a personal relationship with Jesus Christ and believers wounded by life's difficulties. We are God's search party, meant to be a combined partnership to find the lost and hurting and bring them into the fullness of life and fellowship with Jesus Christ. This search requires that believers become partners, first with God's Holy Spirit and then with other Christians, joining in God-directed efforts in ministry to others. This search requires that we join one another in prayer and outreach.

Dr. Yonggi Cho is a powerful and deeply spiritual leader, but the church's impact cannot be credited solely to one man or even to one system of organization. The 720,000-member Yoido Full Gospel Church is an army of believers joined to one another in obedient partnership with our good God of power and grace.

Few churches—perhaps no others—will reach the numbers that crowd into YFGC every Sunday and pack its home cell groups through the week, but if more churches would apply the principles of this church's success, we would see many more millions of people brought into the kingdom of God. YFGC's example is a challenge to us all.

Starting on page 181 you will find discussion questions on the introduction and on each chapter. These questions aid participants in applying the basic principles and practices in their own daily lives, and can be used by your church's pastoral staff, a Sunday school class, in cell group meetings, simply for your own contemplation, or in any other way you deem helpful.

May the reading of this book encourage you to examine this church, adopt its principles wherever possible, and trust God, who has the same power in any age and in any culture.

1

The Early Years

An ancient proverb says, "The beginning is half the whole."[1]
When Yoido Full Gospel Church (YFGC) climbed past a
membership of half a million, many became curious. How did
this church get so big? Were there early times of struggle?

How one begins sets the course for what follows. Before we
can understand the dynamics and major factors of this church's
phenomenal growth, we must first look at its early years and
ask, What can we learn from its history?

A Great Plan to Meet a Great Need

In postwar South Korea conditions were desperate. Thirty-five
years of Japanese occupation and three years of the Korean War
had left the nation in shambles. During the late 1950s, thousands of refugees from the north fled to South Korea, putting an
even greater strain on the devastated country. Bombs and mor-
tar fire had demolished one out of three homes and, in some
areas, four out of five factories. Even the trees were gone, confis-
cated by the Japanese for their war effort or burned as fuel in
desperate times. Jobs were scarce, and every day the Korean
people struggled to survive until the next meal. Poverty and disease were widespread; it is estimated that half the population
had tuberculosis.

The old ways of the formerly strong Buddhist and animist
Korea also lay in desolation. Where had Buddha been during

the nation's darkest hours? What good had it done to tend the graves of ancestors and earnestly pray for their help? What help had the local shamans been?

The stage was set for an incredible move of God. And why not? Already the small number of Christians then in Korea had been praying, crying out to God. They knew that when man has great need, God has a great plan.

A Partnership with Ordinary People

God does not work alone. Instead, to fulfill His plan He chooses to partner with ordinary people. Two unlikely partners God chose in South Korea were Yonggi Cho and Jashil Choi.

No one would have thought Yonggi Cho was destined for greatness in God's kingdom. Cho was reared in a Buddhist home, the first son of eight children. During the Japanese occupation, Cho's mother had shared her one kitchen knife with three other families. Before the Korean War, his father lost most of the land he had owned. By the end of the Korean War, Yonggi Cho had terminal tuberculosis. During that time of struggle, God brought several Christians into his life, and by the time he was twenty, Cho had been born again, miraculously healed, and called into full-time ministry.

> While Yonggi Cho was dying of tuberculosis, he was visited by Yongae Kim, the Christian teenage friend of his older sister, Hyunsook. It was this friend who first gave him a clear presentation of the gospel, left a Bible with him, and visited him repeatedly.
>
> Later, temporarily recovered, Cho went to a revival with speaker Ken Tice, a Navigator missionary. Cho became Tice's interpreter and was introduced to Assemblies of God missionary Lou Richards. During this time Cho was healed and made a definite decision to receive Jesus Christ as his Lord. It was Richards who helped Cho go to Bible school in Seoul.

In 1956 Yonggi Cho, along with more than a dozen other hopefuls, entered Seoul's two-year Full Gospel Bible Institute, operated by the Assemblies of God. Cho ranked at the top of his class and busily pursued theological studies. By 1957 Yonggi had proven himself a diligent student, especially adept in English. Because of his expanded English vocabulary, Yonggi served as an interpreter for American teachers and guest lecturers. His job as interpreter paid for his tuition and board (his Buddhist parents, then living in Korea's southern city of Pusan, would not help him financially).

Jashil Choi's story was different from Cho's. As a child, she had first heard the gospel from the preacher of a tent revival. Yet, Jashil did not turn to Jesus Christ until her marriage grew cold and her oldest child suffered an untimely death. After her Buddhist husband left her with three children, Jashil, a middle-aged midwife, almost committed suicide. Then she heard the same preacher she had met as a child, only this time she turned her heart fully to God. She soon developed an ardent prayer life and then, with her savings and three growing children, went to Seoul to attend Bible school. It was there Jashil met young Yonggi Cho.

During the winter of 1957, Yonggi grew desperately ill with a severe case of the flu. For fifteen days Jashil Choi nursed him and prayed for him, resulting in a strong bond between them.

Because of the difference in their ages and the fact that Yonggi's parents lived so far away, Yonggi called Jashil "Mom," and she called him "Son." Little did they know then that Jashil would become Yonggi's mother-in-law when he would later marry her daughter Grace.

The two unlikely partners, Yonggi and Jashil, often went together with a group of students to nearby Pagoda Park to sing and preach the gospel. Jashil respected Yonggi's intellect and dedication to the gospel, and Yonggi admired her unwavering persistence in prayer.

A Church in a Tent

A few years before, Jashil had been given ten thousand square feet of land next to a cemetery—a gift from a grateful official whom she and her husband had helped during lean times. The property was in a poor, outlying area of Seoul known as Bulkwangdong. After she graduated from Bible school, Jashil applied to work in a nearby orphanage but was rejected for another worker. So Jashil purchased a tattered military tent, set it up on her property, and started a church.

Jashil did not want to be the pastor. She wanted Yonggi Cho

to become pastor while she served as his supportive coworker. The church had not yet started and there was no congregation. Jashil hardly had enough money to support her children, much less a pastor.

Jashil asked Yonggi Cho to preach the opening service on May 15, 1958. Only five people heard Yonggi's first sermon in the tent church in Bulkwangdong: Jashil Choi, her three children, and a farmer's aging widow. Yonggi's pulpit was a stack of wooden apple crates covered by a thin cloth. While he spoke, the tired old woman went to sleep and started snoring. Yonggi almost walked out.

A Summer of Evangelistic Crusades

In the summer of 1958, my father, John Hurston, and Pastor-Evangelist Ralph Bird went to preach in week-long tent campaigns in South Korea's six major cities.[2]

Dad and Mom had already gained distinction for eight years of missionary work in Liberia, West Africa. The president of that country had even knighted Dad and funded him in a presidential inaugural salvation-and-healing campaign that took the gospel into the country's coastal and interior cities, towns, and villages. While on furlough from Liberia, Dad was asked to preach in the Korean Global Conquest crusades, leaving my mother and me in the States.

Two interpreters helped during those crusades, one of whom was Yonggi Cho. Yonggi interpreted frequently for Dad and also spoke in the early morning prayer meetings. The pace was fairly rapid with four daily services, but Dad and Yonggi often talked between the meetings.

One of the young Korean preacher's questions was about divine healing. Even though he had been healed of tuberculosis, Yonggi had heard guest lecturers at the Bible institute say that the age of miracles had passed with the last of the twelve apostles. Divine healing and miracles, they contended, were no longer needed.[3] However, Yonggi had also read a book on healing by Oral Roberts, who pointed to passages in the Bible that supported healing in current times. Yonggi asked Dad whether he thought healing and miracles were for today. He also asked, "What would happen if I prayed for someone, and that person wasn't healed?" Dad responded by telling him of healings he had witnessed in West Africa. "Healing," Dad emphasized, "is vital to God's present-day plan."

Soon, dramatic conversions and healings began to take place in those summer crusade meetings. One old Korean man had been tortured by the Japanese for a minor disobedience. The Japanese had thrust a chopstick into each of the man's ears, bursting his eardrums. He had not been able to hear for fifteen years. During a crusade service he suddenly started hearing again. The next day the old gentleman brought all his family members to the meetings, including his grandchildren. That entire family became born-again Christians. Yonggi told Dad, "Now I believe in the healing ministry more than ever!" Before the tent crusades were over and Dad returned to America, Yonggi himself was praying for the sick.

Desperate Prayer for Desperate Problems

After the excitement of the tent crusades, Yonggi reluctantly returned to pastor the tent church in poverty-ridden Bulk-wangdong. Several times he tried to quit and even headed to the central train station to buy a ticket for Pusan and home. But his faithful ministry partner, Jashil Choi, would follow after him, begging him to obey God no matter how hard it was. He never boarded the train.

Yonggi and Jashil struggled to get the new church on its feet, daily throwing themselves upon God in desperate prayer. One member recalls seeing Yonggi praying in the tent on a cold winter day. Wrapped in a straw rice mat, he would cry out loudly to God and then pray in tongues.

Yonggi and Jashil were often discouraged and desperate. During this time they learned a vital truth: Desperation, when turned over to God, becomes a divine channel for His blessings. Man's problems, when yielded to God, are His opportunities to show His love and power.

Every morning at 4:30 they would use an empty gas container as a bell to summon believers to pray. The rest of the day they visited in the homes of their poor community, ministering and praying with any who would allow it. Meanwhile, at almost any hour of the day, people were praying in the tent. Many joined in teams, some with Yonggi, others with Jashil, to go to homes and pray for the sick and receptive.

The Beginning of Growth

Then the Holy Spirit began to break things loose. A man who had had palsy for seven years was healed. A local shaman renounced her witchcraft, accepted Jesus Christ as Lord, and burned her idols. A well-known alcoholic was converted. News of all this spread in the small community, and church attendance started to climb.

Yonggi and Jashil held their first water baptismal service in a nearby river on March 15, 1959. Two months later, they added another tent, this one sided with wooden planks. Within two years, the congregation had grown to two hundred.

The 1958 summer crusades had deeply affected Dad, and the desperate need in Korea moved him to return there instead of to Liberia. Dad had always said that missionaries were like scaffolding: Once the work was built, it was time to move on. Leadership should come from believers in the host country. So Dad turned his growing church in Monrovia over to a Liberian pastor and boarded a cargo ship for Korea, this time with Mom and me. He knew that God had called him to South Korea. Dad often said, "The most important thing is to be God's person at God's time in God's place."

The winter of 1960 was bitterly cold. The December day our ship finally pulled into Korea's Inchon Harbor, widowed mothers lined the gangplank, squatting beside worn crates, trying to sell their wares to new arrivals. Men mutilated in the war pulled themselves around on homemade carts. War orphans roamed nearby streets as beggars and pickpockets.

We finally found a truck to take us the thirty miles into Seoul. The truck cab was so small my father had to ride in the back on top of our boxes and barrels. As we drove, I gazed out the window. The mountains we passed were filled with shanty towns—houses made of pasteboard walls and roofs created with beaten beer cans discarded by the American military. The countryside was filled with people in desperate need of the saving love and message of Jesus Christ.

That winter I went with my mother to the church in Bulkwangdong that met under the old tent. The small coal stoves scattered in the center of the tent provided little heat, so I huddled close to my mother as I watched and listened the best I could to the preaching of the thin but fiery Yonggi Cho. At the time I did not think of him as a spiritual giant. To a seven-year-old, he was just a young Korean minister with whom my wise father spent so much time talking and praying.

Korea required that each young man serve three years of military duty. When Yonggi's time came, he asked Dad to pastor the tent church until his discharge; he, too, knew that God brings the right people at the right time and place to further His plan.

So we parked our thirty-two-foot silver Spartan trailer near the tent. Dad and Mom went regularly to the early morning prayer meetings and made home visits during the day. They visited many people, some in cement block homes, but most in houses made of pasteboard. Wherever they went, their message was the same: Jesus came to save, bless, and meet needs.

Dad held a revival in the local marketplace, this time with a strong focus on the Holy Spirit. He returned one day marveling, "It was like what you'd imagine at Pentecost! I felt such a strong presence of the Holy Spirit. This morning I walked among nearly eight hundred in prayer. Each person I heard was speaking in tongues. It was a touch of heaven."

Within a short time, the congregation grew to six hundred.

God's Provision

The growth of the church required more funds and larger facilities, difficult to acquire in a war-torn country. But if we were to reach more people in the city of Seoul, it was necessary to have a much larger and more centrally located facility.

Even before we knew our needs, God was arranging provision. Before Dad came to Korea the second time, God had spoken to him about building a large church in Seoul. So Dad had already shipped a prefabricated building to Korea to serve as a sanctuary for a church. That portable building was purchased with funds from the Global Conquest program of the Assemblies of God, the Voice of Healing in Dallas, and other donors.[4] During the months Dad was interim pastor at the tent church in

Bulkwangdong, he also oversaw construction of that prefabricated building in the central area of the city known as Sodaemoon, which means "West Gate." While Dad was praying one day, he knew this was the site God was providing.⁵

The Korean army gave Yonggi a medical discharge after seven months of service. He had a bleeding hernia (which was later healed). Dad asked Yonggi and Jashil to join him at the new facility. It would be the larger and more central facility they had been praying for.

Some missionaries protested, for they felt Yonggi was too young, inexperienced, and proud for such responsibility. Besides, they contended, the tent church had been an independent work, and they wanted to preach themselves in the new structure. But Dad prevailed, and both Yonggi and Jashil moved with him.

In September 1961, we began the new church by holding morning and evening healing crusades in a tent on a lot next to the construction site. Moving to Sodaemoon was like starting over, for many from the first congregation could not afford the long bus ride to the new location.

During this time we saw repeated answers to prayer. Jashil's Buddhist husband returned and became a fervent Christian, and their broken family was finally restored. Yonggi's Buddhist parents also came to a saving faith in Jesus Christ. In later years his father, Duchun Cho, would serve as an elder in the church.

A Vision for the Largest Church

Yonggi's vision for the church grew during this time. He and Dad often talked of how they sensed God leading them to build the largest church in Korea. One day, at Dad's prompting, they visited what was then the largest church in Korea, with a membership of about ten thousand. Yonggi stepped off the size of that sanctuary in meters, while Dad stepped it off in yards. Much to their surprise, their new sanctuary was even wider. That simple act of comparison excited them; they wanted to work in cooperation with the vision they knew God had birthed in their hearts.

God's hand continued to be on the new facility. On October 15, 1961, we held the first service in the new 1,500-seat auditorium, then called the Full Gospel Revival Center. The building was packed. In the middle of the service, there was a flurry of commotion in the center aisle. A crippled beggar, who had pulled himself to the church on a wooden cart, got up and started to walk. Healings were frequent in the early days of the church.

At this point, Yonggi Cho had been licensed to preach (but not yet ordained) by the Korean Assemblies of God. Since Assemblies of God preachers in Korea had to be ordained to pastor a church, Dad served as pastor of the new church for the first year with Yonggi as associate pastor.[6] Since Dad was not fluent in the language, Yonggi did most of the preaching.

By 1962, nearly four years after the church began, a core of more than twelve hundred believers formed the congregation. In April of that year, the Korean Assemblies of God ordained Yonggi Cho. Amid the protests of some, Dad stepped down as senior pastor, becoming a missionary advisor to the Korean pastor. Dad knew he had to work in cooperation with what God was doing. He would speak on Sunday nights, and during the week he would plant churches in other cities. On May 12, 1962, the church's name was changed to Full Gospel Central Church.

A Partnership with Laypeople

Yonggi Cho and Jashil were students of Scripture, and they noted that Jesus did not choose to work alone. It impressed them that after a night of prayer, Jesus chose twelve disciples (Luke 6:12–13). He later sent out the Seventy to spread the good news (Luke 10:1). The men Jesus chose were not religious leaders but ordinary people with hearts for God.

A growing church requires growing partnership with layleaders, so Yonggi Cho followed Jesus' pattern. He prayerfully appointed layleaders, and soon a growing group of deacons, deaconesses, and elders joined in ministry. Jashil focused her efforts on the deaconesses and was soon training teams in home visitation. Her daughter Grace led one of the choirs, part of an emerging music ministry. By 1963, five years after the church began, attendance had grown to eighteen hundred, and a balcony and three-story front were added to accommodate the thriving congregation. One observer said: "These believers have rid themselves of the idea that preaching is done only by pastors. They have become partners in ministry who go out, pray, and spread the gospel."

The work of these laypeople was significant. However, Yonggi Cho still tried to carry much of the ministry load. After a physical collapse in 1964, he realized that he was still trying to do too much by himself, so he started the home cell groups. Later that year, our family returned to America for two years of missionary furlough.[7]

Expanding Services and Ministries

On March 1, 1965, seven years after the church started, nearly three thousand tried to crowd into the Sodaemoon sanctuary to see their pastor marry Grace, the daughter of coworker Jashil. The church, with a reputation for fervent prayer and God's healing power, continued to grow. By May 1965, two morning services could not accommodate the growing crowds, so a third morning service was added. When Yonggi Cho spoke at a meeting in the city of Taegu, policemen were needed to control the crowds.

By February 1966, attendance reached nearly five thousand in the three Sunday morning services. In April of that year, the Korean Assemblies of God elected Yonggi Cho as their superintendent, a position he was to hold for several years. A fourth and fifth story were added to the building. By the time Grace gave birth to the first of Cho's three sons, between twenty and thirty families were joining the church each week.

Soon the church was expanding into various kinds of media. In February 1967, the first copy of the church's monthly magazine, *Shinangge* (meaning "World of Faith"), came off the presses. It is now the most popular religious monthly magazine in Korea.

International demand for Yonggi Cho's ministry grew. In April of that year he spoke in Westminster Abbey in London at an event sponsored by a Christian university association. Later that year, he preached in Japan and Taiwan. By this time, Jashil Choi was also occasionally ministering overseas. As Cho traveled, the missionary vision of the church blossomed.

Dad, Mom, and I returned to Korea in 1967. Patterns of partnership ministry were set. Yonggi Cho preached salvation and healing in the multiple morning services, and Dad preached on receiving and moving in the fullness of the Holy Spirit in the two evening services. The church continued to grow.

On January 1, 1967, shortly before our family returned to Korea, Cho wrote:

"Right now we are using the fourth floor to accommodate the overflowing crowds of Sunday school children and the youth. On the fifth floor we already built one big room for the church library and literature program. I have started to publish our church magazine and have hired two workers already. . . . Our work here is growing, and we need your hands of cooperation very much. All the tears of sowing have passed away, and right now I am having the full joy of wonderful reaping. So come quickly and join with us for this victory and great harvest! Only you and we know how many tears we had to shed to see this day."

More people wanted to hear what God was saying through this fast-growing work. Yonggi Cho started weekly radio broadcasts during that time, laying the groundwork to later launch into television. Full Gospel Central Church was learning how to influence others and expand the kingdom of God. Yonggi Cho soon received the first of several honorary doctorates, becoming affectionately known as Dr. Cho.

At the end of 1967, nine years after the Seoul church began in a tent, its membership had climbed from 5 people to a congregation of 7,750, and untold thousands had been born again, healed, and filled with the Holy Spirit.

In 1968 the church reported nearly 8,000 members and 150 home cell groups. They already had won untold numbers of spiritual victories, but challenges remained. The greatest problem was providing enough room to hold the growth; even multiple services could not accommodate all the people. Latecomers had to stand outside and peer through open windows or sit in the cement parking lot and hear the service over loudspeakers. Children's and youth ministries were burgeoning, as well as the Women's Fellowship. The Men's Fellowship began, soon followed by men's cell groups.

Dad had been president of Full Gospel Bible School (from which Dr. Cho had graduated when it was yet an "institute"). In 1969, Dad began night Bible school classes at the Sodaemoon church to train the church's deacons and deaconesses who wanted to enter full-time ministry but worked during the day. As a girl of sixteen, I taught English conversation to a classroom filled with aspiring pastors. (Among my students was Jashil Choi's husband, soon to enter the ministry.) Not only was the church growing in numbers, but there was also an increasing desire for greater commitment to the Lord and His service.

Great Sacrifices for Great Needs

Dr. Cho and the congregation were soon to discover that growth can be painful. It was obvious that they needed larger facilities, and there was no practical way to continue adding onto the Sodaemoon building. Through the help of Ilsuk Cha, then a vice-mayor of Seoul, Dr. Cho and the leaders found a spot on Yoido Island.

Yoido is a man-made island. Although Seoul was developing it as the newest part of the city, Yoido was not an inviting place. Jetties held back the surging waters of the Han River on all sides of the barren island. Construction was sparse and public transportation limited. Nevertheless, the church bought land on Yoido and held a ground-breaking service there on April 6, 1969.

Some church members weren't ready for the move. They weren't sure if they wanted to develop in a brand-new part of town. Perhaps Dr. Cho and the elders had made a serious mistake. The building fund remained almost as bare as the island.

Something had to happen or they would never have the new church they needed. After several months, the church had less than 1 percent of the money required to build on Yoido Island. To help raise money, they planned to build condominiums near the edge of the Yoido property. That way, they reasoned, money from condominium sales would be put into the building fund and the new sanctuary would have a built-in congregation.

At first, Dr. Cho's wife, Grace, objected: "Why when God told you to build the church, are you now building condominiums? Do what God tells you in the way He tells you, and He will send you the needed money."

But the condominiums were built anyway. Dr. Cho and Grace sold their own house, gave the profit to the building fund, and moved into one of the condominiums; even so, few others wanted to live so far from downtown Seoul. By 1971, 90 percent of the condominiums sat vacant; a financial cure had turned into a disaster. Human solutions, apart from God's guidance, only bring more problems.

Problems mounted as months turned into years. After the Arab oil embargo, the cost of building materials went up. Banks refused to give big loans, and many church members who had pledged money lost their jobs. At the lowest point, one company sued the church for unpaid bills. The construction of the sanctuary halted; the building did not even have a roof. Many nights Dr. Cho went to the gaping structure, spread a straw mat on the bare cement floor, and prayed in desperation.

God's answer came in the most unexpected way. During a service, an elderly woman slowly made her way to the front. Dr. Cho looked down in surprise as she held up her worn silver rice bowl, a pair of chopsticks, and a spoon.

"I have no money to give," she explained in a reedy voice. "All I have is this used silver rice bowl, a pair of chopsticks, and a spoon. I want to give them to the Lord's work. I can put my rice on cardboard and eat with my hands."

At first Dr. Cho refused. How could he take such a precious gift from a poor old woman? But she insisted, "You must take them. They are all I have, and I must give something to help finish our church."

Then a businessman stood to his feet in the back of the church, tears filling his eyes. He offered to buy the rice bowl, chopsticks, and spoon for more than a thousand dollars. Soon others followed in sacrificial giving.

Some sold houses and moved to smaller apartments and gave the profit to the building fund. Women cut their long hair and sold it to wig companies and gave the money to the church.

Money began to pour in and the crisis was averted. At the end of 1972, fourteen years after five people attended the first service in the tent church, membership figures broke the ten thousand barrier. Months later, on August 19, 1973, the church held their first worship service in the new Yoido sanctuary, later becoming Yoido Full Gospel Church.[8]

Valuable lessons were learned in those early years. But the battle was not over. In many ways, it had just begun. (See Appendix 1: The Later Years.)

Yonggi Cho and Jashil Choi, 1961.

The John Hurston family, 1960.

Praying for the sick during the 1958 crusades.
Above: Ralph Bird, Yonggi Cho, and John Hurston.
Below: John Hurston and an interpreter.

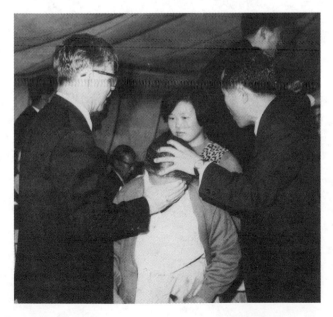

The "tent" church in Bulkwangdong in 1961, after the original tent was expanded.

The overflow crowd on dedication day of the Sodaemoon church in 1961.

A recent picture of Yonggi Cho's parents.

Some of Yonggi Cho's family (from left to right): Yong Chan (Cho's younger brother), Cho's mother and father, Hyesook (Cho's eldest sister), and Kehun (Yong Chan's wife).

2

The Ministry of Prayer

I was only seven years old at the time, but even now I have vivid memories of the tent church at Bulkwangdong. When it rained, the people placed buckets in strategic areas to catch the water that ran through the holes. There was no flooring but the ground. Yet, even in that humble situation, members considered God holy and worthy of praise and their church a holy place.

I was especially struck by what I saw the first time I went with my mother to the tent church. Those who came early were already praying, sitting cross-legged on straw mats spread over bare ground. Heads were bowed as they gently rocked back and forth, praying to God in low tones. Although they had few material possessions, they were quick to thank God for what they did have. Even as a little girl it was easy to sense the precious presence of the Holy Spirit in that place.

Almost thirty years later, I went to that church again, this time for a research visit at the newly expanded YFGC complex. It was 8:40 on a weekday morning, and I was hurrying down a spacious hall to an appointment, my heels clicking on the terrazzo floor. Suddenly I was aware of that same spirit of prayer that had filled the tent church so many years before. I passed a cleaning woman dusting a banister leading up a set of stairs. Her head was bowed and her lips moved silently as she worked. Her prayerful reverence caused me to slow my busy pace; a holy hush permeated the corridor.

I quietly opened the door to one of the staff pastors' large offices. Inside were twelve desks staffed by ministers responsible for specific geographic areas. They sat at their desks, heads bowed and eyes closed, praying softly.

I quietly backed out and closed the door. I went to another large office. Once more I found staff pastors in prayer, some in slightly louder tones. It was the same in the third office and in the fourth.

Later I found my friend, a staff pastor with whom I had the appointment. He explained, "We always start our day with one hour of prayer in each pastoral office. We will be busy ministering to people the rest of the day, but ministry to God in prayer and worship comes first. Then we can be effective in ministry to others. Honor God, and He will honor you."

Prayer as a Way of Life

Prayer is integrated in the everyday activities of the lives of YFGC members. Almost every service, Cho mentions the importance of a daily family altar. He encourages families to pray and read the Word of God together daily and often refers to his own family's devotions and prayer. Scripture passages and devotional thoughts for the family altar are printed in *The Citizen's Newspaper,* the church's daily publication.

A young man from a poor family told of the inspiration he received through his family's daily altar. Through reading the Bible and praying with his family, he realized that God loved him and wanted good things for his life. He became diligent in school, even doing his homework "as unto God." His grades soared. Even though he was in a little-known high school, he received a rare full scholarship for four years to Seoul National University, the "Harvard" of Korea. He said, "The beginning point was our family altar. My whole life changed because of family prayer and devotions."

Another time believers pray for one another is at special events. YFGC reminds believers that the writer of Proverbs said, "In all your ways acknowledge him, and he will make your paths straight" (Proverbs 3:6). The believer is to "pray in the Spirit on all occasions with all kinds of prayers and requests" (Ephesians 6:18).

Special occasions for prayer in Korea include the celebration

of a baby's hundredth day after birth, a marriage, the dedication
of a business or a building, a sixtieth birthday, or any other significant milestone. Believers make it a practice to have other
Christians join them for these special events, primarily to pray
and bless the occasion. No lighter side of a party begins until
there has first been a Scripture reading and prayer.

I went to one dedication service for a warehouse under construction. As soon as the central beam was up, a businessman
asked a YFGC staff pastor and fellow Christians to join him. We
stood in a circle on the bare cement floor in the middle of the
warehouse frame. After reading Deuteronomy 28:8, the staff
pastor talked of the blessings of God to those who are obedient.
We then bowed our heads and said a prayer of blessing over the
warehouse. The businessman later commented, "We might have
looked a little strange to the people around us, but I don't care.
God is the source of all I have. Even before it's finished, I
wanted that warehouse dedicated to Him and His purposes. God
blesses those who look to Him in simple faith."

The people at YFGC believe that we are to approach God in
prayer with reverence. The psalmist instructed, "Worship the
Lord in the splendor of his holiness; tremble before him, all the
earth" (Psalm 96:9). Members consider their church a holy place
of prayer. As Christ said, "My house will be called a house of
prayer" (Matthew 21:13). So when people enter the sanctuary
early, they do not talk but quickly find a seat, bow their heads,
and pray quietly.

A common attitude at the church is reflected in the words of
Staff Pastor Changpyo Yim[1]: "More important than all the
growth-producing practices at our church is the presence and
reality of spiritual empowerment. As we join with God in prayer
for ourselves and for others, He gives us His power, wisdom, and
strength."

It may surprise some to learn that YFGC has no annual seminar on prayer, nor does it have a specific prayer minister on
staff. The importance the congregation places on prayer is best
shown by the many occasions for prayer in worship services, by
the ardent prayer meetings, and in the church's prayer retreat,
Prayer Mountain. Prayer is practiced more than discussed, done
more than explained. There are few times when prayer is more
practiced than during prayer meetings.

Early Morning Prayer Meetings

Prayer is present in every worship service but is especially highlighted in early morning prayer meetings and all-night prayer services. Early morning prayer has been the norm for all Korean Christians since a Presbyterian pastor began it in the Great Prayer Revival of 1907.[2] Some participants refer to the example of David: "In the morning, O Lord, you hear my voice; in the morning I lay my requests before you and wait in expectation" (Psalm 5:3).

Others refer to the examples of Jesus and the apostles, who often went early to the temple to pray (see Luke 21:37–38; John 8:2; Acts 5:21).[3] Most Korean church bells—such as those in YFGC's earlier days—ring at dawn, with the faithful gathering by five o'clock to listen to a faith-inspiring sermon and to pray. They return home at six, eat a quick breakfast, and leave for work.

I found that it's not any easier for Koreans to get up early than for anyone else. It can be a struggle. Once in the tent church Yonggi Cho arrived a few minutes late for early morning prayer, still wiping sleep from his eyes. As he walked to the podium to preach before leading the congregation in prayer, people started to laugh. He had put on his shirt and jacket, but had forgotten to change his pajama trousers.

Dr. Cho says, "Early morning prayer service requires you to deny your desires and yield to God." One young member explained, "When I or someone I know has a problem, or when I am simply wanting to grow closer to Jesus, I like to covenant with my Senior Partner, the Holy Spirit, to go to early morning prayer thirty days in a row. I have seen God do many marvelous things when I pray persistently in this way."

All-Night Prayer

When the church was still in a tent, a few destitute and sick people sometimes prayed all night. After all, Jesus himself, our supreme example, prayed through the night (Luke 6:12).

The first regular all-night prayer service did not begin until the summer of 1972. It was a desperate time for the church. The few funds they had been able to scrape together to build the much needed, larger Yoido facility were not even enough to finish the steel framework.

"Look at that thing they call a house of prayer," passersby sneered. "They talk about the power of God, but He can't even give them enough to finish a building."

So a determined few met one Tuesday night to pray in the basement of an apartment building nearby. Since buses did not run late from the newly developed Yoido Island, and the government-enforced curfew extended from midnight till four o'clock in the morning, those who came had to stay all night.

Attendance at the Tuesday all-night prayer meeting grew. According to Yongchan Cho, former president of YFGC's Youngsan Seminary, "Those who stayed for prayer quickly discovered they were too tired to work on Wednesdays, so Dr. Cho suggested that they switch to Friday night. This allowed people to rest on Saturday after a half day of work."[4]

By the time God provided the finances needed to move into the Yoido sanctuary in August 1973, all-night Friday prayer had become a habit for many. The long distance from the Yoido facility made participation in early morning prayer too difficult for most. So, to adapt to changing needs and schedules, the staff put more emphasis on all-night prayer. Even when the government lifted its curfew in 1980, all-night prayer services continued.

Testimonies of answered prayer grew. By 1977, the main sanctuary was overflowing on Friday nights, so a Wednesday all-night service was added. Since 1980, services have been held from ten at night until four the next morning each day of the week except Sunday. Wednesdays and Fridays have the greatest attendance—up to twenty-five thousand.

At first the all-night prayer meeting was like a typical worship service, with simply more time given to praying, and testimonies being focused on answered prayer. But it was soon evident that the format for the all-night prayer meeting should be even more varied.

Most layleaders come to all-night prayer one night a week, often bringing an unbeliever with needs.[5] "I love to come to all-night prayer," said one member. "I try to bring at least one non-Christian neighbor or acquaintance with me, especially someone who has a personal problem or need. When they hear the faith inspiring sermons and experience the powerful

---

All-Night Prayer Meeting Format

9:00 —People start gathering for a time of meditative prayer and worship in song.

10:00—The official service starts. This segment is similar to the Sunday worship service, with important exceptions. The designated staff pastor preaches an hour-long, faith-inspiring sermon, often with focus on personal needs. The congregation then joins in concert prayer, lifting personal petitions to God.

12:45—Short break.

1:00—A staff pastor leads the congregation in concert prayer focusing on specific matters of local, national, and international concern. According to one church member, "This is our time for prayer with pointed objectives, when we join in verbal prayer for important matters. I have seen many changes in the land of Korea when we pray this way. God loves to hear our prayers."

2:00—People share testimonies of answered prayer. This is known as the most faith-building segment of the all-night service.

2:30—The people enjoy congregational singing and prayer. Since they have just heard testimonies of answered prayer, their songs and petitions are spirited and lively. Anticipation of God's working in each situation is high.

3:30—There is another short worship service, replacing the early morning prayer meeting from earlier days.

4:30—Believers raise their hands and shout a loud "Hallelujah!" Then they pour into the streets and head home. Many manage a couple of hours of sleep before going to work.

---

prayer, they begin to sense that God is real. When they hear the testimonies of God's answers to prayer, they begin to desire for God to touch them as well. Just last week, I brought a friend who wouldn't have come except that she had a problem with indigestion. By the end of the all-night prayer meeting, she was healed. That next Sunday she became a Christian. Now she's bringing friends to our cell group and has already taken one other person to an all-night prayer meeting with her. There's nothing like the power of the Holy Spirit in prayer."

Members and the pastoral staff encourage anyone with difficulties or problems to participate in prayer meetings, telling what God has done in the lives of others who have participated in the meetings. Regular participation in prayer meetings is highly valued by the congregation, mainly because they have seen how God through prayer has benefited so many lives.

As one cell leader has said, "Even though my physical body is tired after all-night prayer, the spirit inside me is much stronger. I would rather come to all-night prayer than sleep. The benefits are eternal."

An Awareness of the Spirit Realm

Fundamental to the church's prayer life has always been its belief in the absolute reality of the unseen realm. This spirit world has two unequal opposing sides. Jesus Christ, with infinitely greater power, rules the kingdom of God and oversees His angelic beings. Satan rules the kingdom of darkness, filled with his demonic hordes. These two kingdoms are constantly at war, with individual souls the prime battleground.[6] The only way for the believer to overcome in this battle is to pray and carefully obey the Word of God. Prayer is one of the believer's weapons in the spirit realm.

Even from the church's beginning, awareness of the spirit realm permeated prayer and ministry. Grace Cho was a teenager when the church began under the tent. Her part in those worship services was to play the small Yamaha organ donated by two American soldiers.

"I still remember those days," Sister Cho told me. "So many poor and crazy people came to our tent church. One wild acting woman who came was really sick. Her eyes were fixed in a distant gaze, her behavior was irrational, and she complained of constant pain. Nobody had been able to help her. When my mother and Yonggi prayed for her, they sensed she had a demon, so they started casting it out. They repeatedly demanded, 'Go out in the name of Jesus!'

"Then two different voices spoke out of her. One was a man's voice and the other that of a woman. They seemed to be fighting each other. My mother and Yonggi prayed several hours for her. Then, during a time of intense prayer, she suddenly collapsed limp on the floor. When she finally awoke, her gaze was clear, her behavior normal, and she no longer had any pain. At that point she readily received Jesus Christ as her Lord and Savior. She was so glad to be delivered and completely healed."

Empowerment of the Holy Spirit

One guiding Scripture verse for members is Zechariah 4:6—"Not by might nor by power, but by my Spirit, says the Lord Almighty." YFGC teaches that the power of Pentecost—the baptism in the Holy Spirit—is distinct from salvation. Such was the case for the early Christians on the Day of Pentecost (Acts 2:1–4), the Samaritans who responded to Philip's preaching (Acts 8:14–17), and the twelve Ephesian men to whom Paul spoke (Acts 19:1–7). In those instances they first believed in Jesus and were later baptized in the Holy Spirit. Salvation and one's receiving the baptism in the Spirit can happen at the same time (though not necessarily).

In one of his sermons, Dr. Cho said, "It is through the Holy Spirit that we are drawn to Jesus Christ and sealed in our new birth. But there is more to the person of the Holy Spirit than that. He also desires to fill you with His fullness, to baptize you with His power, and to have daily fellowship with you."

Many believers pray long hours, asking God to give them the baptism in the Holy Spirit. Each Tuesday morning at ten o'clock there is a special service just for those wanting to receive the baptism in the Spirit. One woman said to me, "The Holy Spirit makes such a difference! I used to be hesitant to share my faith with others, and my prayer life was weak. But after I was baptized in the Holy Spirit, I could easily spend two hours in prayer, interceding for Buddhist neighbors. I am bold now in sharing my faith. It seems a holy fire burns within me."

I knew what she meant. By the time I was nine, I had already received Jesus as my Lord and Savior, but I hungered for more. I wanted the same experience in the Holy Spirit others had. I prayed that God would give me the baptism in His Holy Spirit, but for many months nothing happened. One evening, when the Sodaemoon church had grown to about twelve hundred, I was sitting beside my mother. During concert prayer, as I prayed aloud to God, the warmth of God's presence and joy seemed to flood every part of my being. Suddenly I was so happy! I began to speak in a language I didn't understand.

Then, a clear picture came into my mind. I saw what looked like a demon with his shoulders bent in defeat and head dropped down, trudging slowly away. In that moment I knew that I had received the baptism in the Holy Spirit. I knew it was a defeat of whatever Satan had been trying to do to me and that my prayer life would never be the same again.

When Dad and Yonggi Cho heard what had happened, they asked me to share my testimony from the platform. Cho interpreted as I spoke. Among the people were one formerly crippled man who had been healed and now walked, a man and his wife once on the verge of divorce whose lives and marriage had been restored, and a widow with a small business that had started prospering. We had all tasted of the baptism in the Holy Spirit, and the experience was sweet.

Praying with Faith from a Pure Heart

The Holy Spirit will not be free to guide and empower in prayer unless we pray with a pure heart, careful to repent first of any known sin. "Who may ascend the hill of the Lord? . . . He who has clean hands and a pure heart . . . He will receive blessing from the Lord" (Psalm 24:3–5).

Dr. Cho highlights this key truth and is first to apply it in his own prayer life. He once told me how he struggled with a bad attitude in a certain situation. "I knew my attitude was sinful," Dr. Cho said, "so I brought it to God and repented. Only then did the situation work out."

A layleader told how she was healed of stomach cancer, but then experienced a relapse. In a time of prayer, the Lord reminded her of her attitude toward her son-in-law. She had been against the marriage from the start. When the young man physically abused her daughter, her heart burned with resentment. When the Lord reminded her of her wrong attitude, she repented, and with Christ's help forgave her son-in-law. She prayed for her healing, and the symptoms lifted. She has not had one trace of cancer in more than seven years. Her son-in-law has since become a Christian and now enjoys a happy marriage with her daughter.

Praying with a pure heart also means praying for the right reasons, not asking "with wrong motives, that you may spend what you get on your pleasures" (James 4:3).

Staff Pastor Jongchul Kim shared that when he was a businessman he prayed that God would prosper his piano business so he could give more to the church. However, God was dealing with him about going into full-time ministry. Jongchul's prayer to get richer so he could give more was really sidestepping God's call. "My family and I are happy now," Jongchul said. "I have the prosperity of being in God's plan for my life and blessing the lives of others. God has also provided for us financially. I have learned that I must pray with the right motive."

Closely linked to praying with the right motive is praying in faith according to God's will. Scripture is clear: "If we ask anything according to his will, he hears us. And if we know that he hears us—whatever we ask—we know that we have what we asked of him" (1 John 5:14–15).

A woman with inoperable cancer came to see Dr. Cho. He reminded her that it was God's will that she be healed, for Scripture states "by His wounds you have been healed" (1 Peter 2:24; see also Isaiah 53:5). Dr. Cho advised her to keep going to prayer meetings, to pray and fast at Prayer Mountain, and to write "By his wounds I have been healed" a hundred times each day.

Desperate, the woman went to Prayer Mountain. The first three days she went through the motions of praying, fasting, attending services, and writing a hundred times a day, "By His wounds I have been healed." On the fourth day, faith rose in her heart. For the first time, she believed she could be healed. She prayed fervently that day and noticed an instant difference in the way she felt.

When she returned from Prayer Mountain, she went to see her doctor. The surprised physician could find no trace of her cancer and pronounced her well.

Specific Prayer

YFGC teaches we are to pray specifically. When Abraham sent his servant to look for a bride for Isaac, the servant prayed that God would send a young woman to the well who would be willing to draw water for his camels. Rebekah came, watered his camels, and traveled back with him to marry Isaac (Genesis 24:42–46,61–67). God answered the specific prayer of Abraham's servant.

When God promised to heal King Hezekiah, the king asked

for a sign: that the shadow cast by the sun would go back ten steps on his stairway. When Isaiah prayed that it would, God answered his specific prayer (2 Kings 20:8–11).

When Bartimaeus approached Jesus, Jesus asked him, "What do you want me to do for you?" (Mark 10:51). Jesus wanted the blind man to state his specific request. Bartimaeus did, and he left with restored sight.

Many YFGC members pray with specific goals in mind, such as the number of people God would have them or their cell groups win to the Lord. Specific goals help the believer focus both prayer and action.

This emphasis on specific praying goes back to the earliest days of Dr. Cho's ministry. He needed three things to minister effectively—a bicycle to do more visitation, a chair to sit in, and a desk to study at—but after six months of praying for these three items, there was no answer. Then he sensed God's prompting to pray specifically. So he began to pray for an American-made bicycle with gears on the side; a mahogany desk from the Philippines; and a large chair with rollers on its legs. Within two weeks of praying this way, a missionary asked young Dr. Cho to help him move some furniture. In appreciation, he gave Dr. Cho his son's used American-made bicycle with gears on the side, a mahogany desk from the Philippines, and a large comfortable chair with rollers.

Putting Feet to Prayer

Even praying specifically, according to God's will, and from a pure heart does not guarantee effective prayer. One must also put feet to one's prayers. Before God answered Moses' cry for help and parted the Red Sea, Moses had to tell the Israelites to go forward and had to raise his staff (Exodus 14:15–16). Before God cured Naaman's leprosy, Naaman had to dip in the Jordan River seven times (2 Kings 5:10,14). Before Jesus raised Lazarus from the dead, the stone had to be rolled from the mouth of the tomb (John 11:38–39,41). Before the man with a withered hand was healed, he had to try to stretch it out (Matthew 12:13).

Effective prayer requires faith, and faith must be accompanied by some type of action, for "faith without deeds is dead" (James 2:20,26).

If a believer prays for the salvation of a person, he should also invite that person to church services and to cell group meetings and give him appropriate Christian literature. If a Christian prays for the healing of a sick friend, the church suggests that he take that friend to Prayer Mountain to pray and fast.

Acts of faith usually include giving. Large wooden chests for tithes and offerings are placed around the main church campus as well as in central locations in the Prayer Mountain chapels. The church encourages those with prayer requests to commit to giving offerings and consistent tithes.

Praying with Persistent Aggressiveness

Another key point is the need to be aggressive in prayer. "After all," one man said, "didn't Jesus say in Matthew 11:12, 'The kingdom of heaven has been forcefully advancing, and forceful men lay hold of it'? Doesn't Jesus give us 'authority to trample on snakes and scorpions and to overcome all the power of the enemy' [Luke 10:19]? Don't we have to be relentless in our prayers to destroy the works of our enemy Satan and establish the kingdom of God in a difficult circumstance?"

For believers at YFGC, prayer is not a casual activity to fill time; it is a serious act of belief in the power of God on one's behalf. In recent years many YFGC members added even more persistence to their prayer for each other with the practice of what they call "Jericho Prayer."

"Jericho Prayer" is based on the Old Testament story of Joshua's conquest of the ancient city of Jericho. Before the walls of Jericho fell, Joshua and the Israelites marched around it once each day for six days, and seven times on the seventh day (Joshua 6:15). In recent years, many YFGC cell leaders have utilized Jericho Prayer—praying for the same person in the same home at the same time seven days in a row. Reports of miraculous answers to Jericho Prayer are frequent, even for unbelievers.

Some have extended this daily prayer and home ministry visit practice to ten days, especially in difficult cases. Staff Pastor Leebu Pak knew of a troubled family whose once studious teenage daughter, Mirah, had suddenly changed. She would even tear off her clothes and run naked in the streets. When they tried to restrain her, she fought viciously and bit them.

The family wasn't Christian, but Pastor Pak and a section leader asked if they could come every day for ten days to pray for Mirah. The distraught mother readily agreed.

The Christians went faithfully every day at the same time. Each time, they prayed, sang a hymn, read a passage of Scripture, shared an exhortation from God's Word, and prayed. Sometimes they had to hold Mirah down to keep her from bolting from the room.

For eight days they saw no change. Then on the ninth day, as they prayed and rebuked demonic forces, Mirah collapsed. When she awoke, she was normal.

"We often pray for deliverance from demonic powers," one leader explained, "because many struggle with the effects of unconfessed sin. Four common sins are adultery, hatred and lack of forgiveness, idolatry, and abortion. Repentance is absolutely necessary, either before or right after God brings healing and deliverance. In Mirah's case, she had tremendous hatred and resentment for her father."

After Mirah's deliverance, she received Jesus as her Lord and Savior. When her mother saw the change, she became born again; her alcoholic father soon followed. Now every family member is a Christian, the father and mother later becoming cell leaders.

Sometimes serious situations require even more persistence in prayer for one another. Once a year, many YFGC subdistricts practice "Daniel Prayer"—meeting at a central home for prayer and worship at a specific time each day for twenty-one consecutive days, since Daniel once fasted for twenty-one days before he received an answer from God (Daniel 10:1–14).

The home chosen usually has a spacious living room. Anyone in that geographic subdistrict is welcome to come as often as he or she likes. Many bring sick friends and acquaintances to these meetings. Usually the subdistrict pastor will minister God's Word before each daily prayer time.

Hyonam Kim knew a woman who was not concerned about spiritual things; however, she had two physical concerns: a stubborn lump near her left shoulder and a daughter with a skin disease. So she agreed to go with Hyonam to one of the Daniel Prayer services. During that meeting, her lump immediately disappeared. Within two days, her daughter's skin cleared. "Her entire family became fervent Christians," Hyonam told me. "God loves for us to pray for one another."

The ministry dynamic of prayer for one another knits YFGC's members together in caring attitudes and actions, including joint prayer and efforts to reach unbelieving friends and neighbors. When there is not a concern for one another, every person and situation suffers.

The impact of YFGC's persistent prayer has been felt in many situations. In 1987 the political situation in Korea was particularly troubled. People feared that violence would flare up before and during the 1988 Olympic Games. Dr. Cho called his senior assistant pastor and asked him to arrange for a few others to meet him the following day for prayer.

His senior assistant pastor called the district pastors, who called their staff pastors. Those staff pastors contacted their senior layleaders, who in turn contacted their home cell leaders. By the following day, more than twenty thousand met with Dr. Cho for prayer. They prayed fervently until late afternoon, asking God for a peaceful solution to the crisis. They commanded Satan to cease his activity, praying for God's peace to be felt by all the Olympic athletes and guests. By the following week, the political storm had calmed. The 1988 Seoul Olympics went off without hindrance, one of the smoothest-running Olympics in history.

Yet all this prayer has affected far more than the Seoul Olympics or even the many individuals who have seen urgent needs met. Prayer by Christians throughout Korea has helped change an entire nation.

By 1900 Korea had only a few Protestant churches. By 1960, South Korea was still staunchly Buddhist and animist, with only 4 percent claiming to be Christian. Thirty years later, in 1990, a reported 30 percent of the South Korean population were born-again Christians.[7] "Prayer," Dr. Cho repeatedly affirms, "is the key to revival. It makes a divine difference."

3

International Prayer Mountain

I was weary. It had been a busy morning, and I had just made the one-hour bus ride from the church to Prayer Mountain, YFGC's prayer retreat. One year before, I had come to Prayer Mountain as a speaker, but now I was tired and in need of some prayer and solitude myself. As I sat resting on a bench near the retreat's entry gate, a warm breeze blew through a familiar cluster of pine trees.

To my left was Prayer Mountain's main auditorium, the 10,000-seat Hallelujah Sanctuary. In front of me lay nearly 330,000 square feet of chapels, dormitories, and buildings spread over ninety acres of hilly land. In an hour I would spend time praying in one of more than three hundred individual prayer grottos, many carved in the side of the nearby hill. But now, as I sat resting, I remembered earlier days.

The Beginnings of Prayer Mountain

I had first gone to Prayer Mountain as a girl of fifteen. At that time this location was the church's cemetery, for in a Buddhist country, a Christian burial has added importance to the Christian. There were few trees in those days. During the Japanese occupation and Korean War, the country had been stripped of its timber. So I had joined my family and church members on Arbor Day, and we had each planted as many pine seedlings as time and energy would allow.

We had laughed as we planted the seedlings. It was fun, but I was also nervous. Just ten miles north of us was the narrow strip of land that served as the Demilitarized Zone between democratic South Korea and communist North Korea. Soldiers from both sides had occasionally fired shots in that narrow strip of what was once farmland. Even though casualties were rare, I felt tense.

Now more than twenty years had passed. North and South Korea talked often of reunification, and relationships between them were friendlier. Some of the pine trees we had planted were now strong and tall; others were bent from the weather. The church had purchased additional land, and since 1973, its retreat site, Prayer Mountain, had been here.

Now an average of three thousand people—including some foreigners—visit Prayer Mountain each day, more than a million a year. Now in this farmland, where conflicts were once fought with guns and tanks, thousands of Christians wage spiritual battles with continual prayer and intercession.

The church cemetery still remains in the same spot, slowly expanding as aging saints leave this world for one far better. After resting, I walked up the path to the middle of the hilly cemetery and stopped before the plot marked "Jashil Choi." Jashil Choi had been Dr. Cho's faithful coworker in earlier days, his most ardent prayer warrior, and the mother of his wife, Grace.

I remember Jashil Choi as a kind woman. My mother first met her on a freezing December day. Jashil took Mother's cold hands in her own and rubbed them until they were warm. Most people remember Jashil Choi as a woman of prayer. When church members talk of how Prayer Mountain began, hers is the name mentioned most often.

In 1972 Jashil Choi started coming often to the church cemetery to pray. Those were the desperate days of financial need that had sparked the first regular all-night prayer meetings. Still the 2.5 million dollars necessary to pay for the church's new Yoido sanctuary were nowhere in sight. Jashil felt the need to leave the city and its distractions and to pray and fast all night long. "After all," she reasoned, "Jesus himself 'went out into the hills to pray, and spent the night praying to God' [Luke

6:12]. Jesus also went into the desert, away from distractions, to fast [see Matthew 4:1–2]."

So Jashil drove one hour to a spot she knew would be isolated, where she could be alone to pray—the church cemetery, set in the midst of hilly fertile farmland near a military installation in the area called Osanri. Jashil was burdened with the church's pressing need for money and prayed loudly through the night.

Yet, the financial problem continued. Soon Jashil made the one-hour drive to the church cemetery every evening and prayed loudly until the early hours of the morning. Jashil, like members of the congregation, believed she was to be like Jesus in all ways: Jesus "offered up prayers and petitions with loud cries and tears to the one who could save him from death, and he was heard because of his reverent submission" (Hebrews 5:7).

The soldiers living in the military installation near the cemetery saw the place in a different light. They complained about Jashil's loud late-night praying. So to absorb the noise, Jashil dug a large hole into the side of a hill and knelt in the hole to pray. She later added a door to cover the hole, creating the first prayer grotto.

Others in the church heard of Jashil's nightly vigils, and a handful of believers sometimes joined her for fervent times of focused prayer and fasting. Jashil soon felt that God wanted the church to buy additional land near the cemetery and develop a prayer retreat, a prayer mountain. Other people facing difficulties and problems needed to be free from the distractions of daily life in order to spend concentrated time with God in prayer and fasting.

Many disagreed. What a foolish idea! Build a prayer and fasting retreat when they didn't even have enough money for the church sanctuary at Yoido? Besides, who would want to pray in that hilly farmland near a cemetery?

God and Jashil prevailed. Six months before the September 1974 dedication of the Yoido sanctuary, the official Prayer Mountain ministry began. They started with the little they had: a few people and a simple cement block house that served as a dormitory and chapel.

Even then people came in increasing numbers, and reports of healings and miracles filtered back to the church and city. Testimonies of healings mounted each day.

Originally the prayer retreat was called Fasting Prayer Mountain, but in recent years the name has changed to International Prayer Mountain. There are now an estimated four hundred to five hundred prayer mountins in Korea. YFGC's International Prayer Mountain is the largest.

Early Testimonies

One of the earlier testimonies from Prayer Mountain came from Insook Lee. After Insook married, doctors told her she couldn't have children; her fallopian tubes were deformed. So Insook went to Prayer Mountain to fast and pray for one week. Four months later she became pregnant. She gave birth to a healthy son. Her second child, a girl, was born eighteen months later. "Persistent prayer and fasting works," says Insook.

Chongmok Chan gave another early testimony. He had developed severe stomach problems. Any time he ate, he would vomit. His pain was so severe that he could lie only on his left side. He could not sleep. When he went to the doctor, his X-ray revealed a severely twisted intestine, probably related to a childhood incident when he had inhaled poisonous fumes from a defective heating system. The doctor wanted to operate to remove the bad section and retie his intestines.

Chongmok did not want surgery, so the doctor prescribed a three-day treatment—which produced no change in his condition. Since becoming a Christian, Chongmok had learned the power of prayer. He went to Prayer Mountain to pray and fast for three days. By the second morning, he felt much better. A month after returning from Prayer Mountain, Chongmok had completely regained his health. He eats normally and has slept well ever since, and his doctor pronounced him well.

Testimonies of healing continue to come from Prayer Mountain. I talked with one elder who worked many years at the prayer retreat. He told me that people who are comfortable and secure in their lives don't come to Prayer Mountain, for people tend not to seek God when things are running smoothly.

"But," he said, "when they are desperate for a solution, then they come. And when they seek God in prayer and fasting, they get answers. That is why they return, bringing needy friends with them. God delights in answering persistent prayer."

Prayer Mountain Staff

Two types of staffs now deal with the growing demands on Prayer Mountain: An extensive administrative staff oversees details and paperwork on overnight visitors, required to register at the Information Checkpoint Gate and receive a name badge. Most who visit on their own come to pray and fast for one to forty days and pay a minimal charge to sleep in one of three main dormitories. A limited cooking staff in the basement cafeteria of Prayer Mountain's Mission Center provides meals for those not fasting. Others on this staff help care for the grounds.

Most importantly, Prayer Mountain has a multiple pastoral staff—at the time of this writing, more than twenty—who focus their attention on ministry. All beginning YFGC staff pastors used to serve one year at Prayer Mountain as their initial training period. Now beginning staff pastors start with ten to twenty-one days of prayer and fasting at Prayer Mountain.

This pastoral staff has a variety of responsibilities. Ordained pastors preach in the services up to three times a week; guest ministers or ordained pastors visiting from the main church campus preach at other services. Licensed ministers on staff collect the offering, then later fan out through the sanctuary to lay hands on people and pray for them. It is this same pastoral staff that receives the Korean translation of the hundreds of foreign prayer requests mailed each week to the church, after they are made the focus of prayer in the main church services.

Prayer Mountain staff members are available for counseling during two set time periods each day. Each staff pastor typically counsels and prays for ten people during each time period, in one of several designated offices. The goal of this time is to pray specifically with that person and to show him or her a more effective way to pray. Couples also come for marital counseling.

Visitors to Prayer Mountain

What do most visitors to Prayer Mountain do? Since "faith comes from hearing the message, and the message is heard through the word of Christ" (Romans 10:17), YFGC considers participation in Prayer Mountain's four daily worship services to be vital. In the words of one woman, "God speaks to me in a special way in the worship services at Prayer Mountain. Not only do I learn more about God's Word, but the sermons inspire my faith to believe in God when I pray. More time is given to song and prayer in those services. The preaching is always powerful, and, afterward, staff pastors often come and pray for us. God does wonderful things when we pray to Him in faith."

Daily Service Schedule	
6:00 A.M.	Early Morning Prayer Service
11:00 A.M.	Midday Service
3:00 P.M.	Holy Spirit Baptism Service
7:00 P.M.	Evening Worship Service
Friday	
10:00 P.M.	All-night Prayer Service

Besides its four daily worship services, Prayer Mountain has special services for Easter, Pentecost, and Thanksgiving. Prayer Mountain also features national and interdenominational ministers' conferences and training seminars. Church groups like YFGC's collegiate Christ's Ambassadors and the Women's Fellowship have annual meetings, often stretching over a week, at Prayer Mountain. These focus on prayer, spiritual growth, and deepening commitment to Jesus Christ.

But most who visit Prayer Mountain are members of the twenty-three geographical districts of the church. Every month each district has a special three-hour prayer and fasting worship service at Prayer Mountain, usually held during the daily late-morning service.

Foreign visitors to Prayer Mountain often comment on the fervency shown during the multiple services. One visiting American minister I know told me that he was first impressed by the sea of buses outside, bringing droves of people into this otherwise isolated farming community. Then he sat in a pew near the back of the sanctuary and observed an entire service.

"Never have I seen people pray with such intensity," he told me. "Sometimes they even rocked back and forth in their seats, crying out to God. There's one large section surrounding the front where people sit on the floor Korean style. I watched as the Prayer Mountain pastoral staff went among the people, laying hands on and praying for each person. Many were visibly touched by the sense of God's presence during this time. I was never more moved with the validity and power of prayer than when gazing at that sacred scene."

Visitors benefit greatly as they participate in daily worship services. Between services, many also pray privately in the more than three hundred individual prayer grottos.

A few of the grottos are reserved for people like Dr. Cho, who often prays in a grotto in preparation for his sermons. The remainder are allotted on a first-come, first-served basis. Individuals find an empty grotto and leave their shoes at the door. The empty grotto is the one without a pair of shoes in front of it.

Many prefer the first grottos built, carved into the sides of surrounding hills. But no matter where it's located, a grotto is not high enough for standing, nor long enough to lie down. All you can easily do in a grotto is kneel.

There are two reasons for these grottos. First, a hole in the ground allows little to distract you, and, second, it affords you the opportunity to pray privately. Another reason is mentioned in Matthew 6:6, the need to pray "in secret."

A Prayer Mountain brochure states, "It is time for you to meet with God. Your life will be changed and blessed with abundant fruit for God as you pray and fast."[1]

One Approach to Planning a Fast

Decide how many meals or days you will pray and fast.

Repent of your sins during the first portion of your fast. Allow the cleansing power of the Holy Spirit to become a reality.

Petition God with specific requests during the second portion of your fast. Be sure to align your desires with God's will.

Resolve to do God's will during the final portion of your fast. Thank God for His answer(s). Then transfer faith into action, and return to your regular schedule with new resolve and faith, continuing to worship God.[3]

The majority of visitors to Prayer Mountain fast as well as pray. Among Korean Christians "fasting prayer" means that you eat nothing solid and drink only water. Prayer Mountain encourages this type of fasting. Some visitors take plastic containers filled with water everywhere they go; they want to be sure to drink enough fluid as they fast.

Basic Principles in Fasting

Begin Gradually. If you are fasting for the first time or are planning a fast of more than five days, it is better to begin gradually. Start by eating only two meals a day, then just one meal a day, decreasing your food intake until you are fasting completely. At times it may be necessary to cleanse the digestive system with an enema.

Participate in Every Worship Service. God speaks through human vessels during each service held at Prayer Mountain. Hearing the Word of God produces faith, and without faith, even prayer during a fast is ineffectual.

Concentrate on Prayer and God's Word. Between worship services during a fast, you are to concentrate on prayer and God's Word and not be distracted. At times when you would otherwise be eating, be sure to pray and read the Bible instead. This is one reason for the prayer grottos.

Drink Plenty of Water. You should drink at least six glasses of water a day, bathe in cool water, and do a limited .amount of light exercise. You should brush your teeth often, as the toxins released while fasting cause bad breath.

End the Fast Properly. Many have damaged the lining in their stomachs by ending a fast improperly. It is especially important to eat lightly after the fast the same number of days that you fasted. The first day after an extended fast, drink juice or soup only. The second day, eat soup, Cream of Wheat, or oatmeal. The third day, eat a large portion of soup or vegetables. Only on the fourth day should you eat a small amount of solid food.

Continue in Prayer. It is important not to overeat, and to continue in persistent prayer even after the fast is concluded. Temptation comes in many forms, and through prayer you can resist.[2]

YFGC points out that fasting has many scriptural references. Jesus himself prepared for public ministry with a forty-day fast (Matthew 4:1–2). "Fasting," one staff pastor declared to me, "benefits the spiritual, the physical, the emotional, and the psychological health of the believer."

In total, YFGC uses nearly forty Bible passages to teach on fasting: Exodus 34:28; Leviticus 16:19–34; Numbers 29:7–12; Judges 20:26; 1 Samuel 1:7–8; 2 Samuel 3:35; 12:16; 1 Kings 19:4–8; 2 Chronicles 20:3; Ezra 8:23; Esther 4:1–3; 4:15–17; Psalms 35:13; 109:22–26; Isaiah 58:6–9; Jeremiah 14:11–12; 36:5–10; Daniel 1:11–21; 6:18; 10:2–3; Joel 1:13–20; 2:12–17; Jonah 3:4–10; Zechariah 7:5; 8:19; Matthew 4:2; 6:16–18; 17:19–20; Mark 2:18–22; 9:29; Luke 4:2; John 4:30–34; Acts 1:14; 9:9; 13:2–3; 14:23.

Expecting Answers to Prayer

Why do people make the effort required to visit Prayer Mountain? People come with a wide assortment of needs, problems, and sicknesses—expecting answers to prayer. According to former Prayer Mountain Staff Pastor Chundong Lee, "The main reason many come to Prayer Mountain is to receive the baptism in the Holy Spirit."

Prayer Mountain staff pastors estimate that between half and two-thirds of Prayer Mountain visitors come to receive the baptism in the Holy Spirit, expecting to speak in tongues. Such was the testimony of Kyongsok Kim, who had an infant granddaughter healed of postnatal brain damage after she and her daughter-in-law prayed and fasted at Prayer Mountain. Kyongsok told me, "There was quite a difference in my prayer life after I received the baptism in the Holy Spirit and spoke in tongues. When the Holy Spirit continually baptizes your life, you cannot help but pray effectively. We brought our infant granddaughter twice to Prayer Mountain. The doctors said she would die from brain damage; even an operation had not been able to save her. But now she is alive and one of the brightest students in her elementary class."

Of the four daily services at Prayer Mountain, one late in the afternoon is specifically for those who want to receive the baptism in the Holy Spirit.

Expecting Answers to Family and Business Problems

People also come to Prayer Mountain with family and business problems. One successful businesswoman came home from a business appointment to find her daughter missing. After calling friends and neighbors and waiting for some time, she contacted the police. The police couldn't help, and none of the girl's friends knew where she was.

The woman did not know what else to do, so she went to Prayer Mountain for three days. During the time she prayed and fasted, her daughter's teacher found an old letter written by the daughter with an address on one page.

After the mother returned from Prayer Mountain, she talked with the teacher and got the address, went to the house, and found her daughter. At first the daughter was angry, but then she softened, breaking down and confessing that she ran away to get the attention of her busy mother. They soon reconciled, and the daughter returned home to a newly attentive mother.

The church also invites all its businessmen to Prayer Mountain for a retreat at the end of each year for a special time of prayer and fasting. One businessman excitedly told me, "Each thing I pray for during that time is answered within a month. Once I prayed that God would help me in my job, and I was promoted the next month. Another year, I asked God to help me start my own company. Because of a bankruptcy, I was able to buy out another business and start my own company. Another time I asked God to help me in my new company. That year contracts quadrupled. God answers persistent prayer."

Expecting Answers to Other Problems

Another major reason people visit Prayer Mountain concerns problems in their churches. Up to four hundred thousand visits each year are made by people from other churches. One Presbyterian pastor who had been struggling to plant a church came for three days of prayer and fasting at Prayer Mountain. He then planted a church near Pusan that has been growing ever since.

People also go to Prayer Mountain with sickness and health problems. Until the recent accelerated influx of visitors, administrative staff kept detailed records of the reasons people come to Prayer Mountain. In 1980, nearly 30 percent of the sick who came to Prayer Mountain had cancer—the most frequently reported illness. Pastors remind visitors, "Nothing is impossible to those who believe."

Yongae Chong had advanced stomach cancer. She was so weak

that her doctor told her she would die just trying to get to Prayer Mountain. Some friends helped her make the journey, and she prayed and fasted for three days. Yongae was healed and remains in good health.

Jongjim Oh was a musician playing an accordion in a nightclub when he discovered he had tuberculosis. When he began coughing up blood, he had to stop working. His Christian mother-in-law said he should go to Prayer Mountain to fast and pray. "If you will confess your sins and believe on the Lord Jesus Christ, He will save and heal you."

Desperate, Jongjim went to Prayer Mountain and followed his mother-in-law's instructions. He stayed for thirty days, fasting one day and eating the next. At the end of that time newly born-again Jongjim went to the hospital for a new X-ray. After an amazed doctor pronounced him completely healed, Jongjim sent the X-ray to Prayer Mountain with this request: "Please keep this at Prayer Mountain to help others believe. God is able. Truly Jesus lives and answers prayer."

In recent years, more and more people who come to Prayer Mountain have had emotional problems.

One example was Chongja Kim. When Chongja's only child died, she sank into a deep depression. After she and her husband had started attending YFGC, things seemed better. Chongja made an initial commitment to Jesus Christ, and though there were still areas of emptiness in her life, she was relatively happy.

Then Chongja bought a lottery ticket. Even though she knew that she had taken an ungodly risk, she prayed to win—that money would have solved their financial needs. When her number lost, Chongja blamed God and dropped out of church and the neighborhood home cell group she attended.

Soon her depression returned, more severe than before. Chongja started hearing strange voices and would bang her head against the wall. She became suicidal. When members of her cell group visited her, Chongja grew angry and told them to leave.

Oddly enough, because of Chongja's problems, her husband's faith grew. He often prayed with Chongja's former cell group leader and other Christians for his wife's emotional well-being. Several times he begged Chongja to go with him to Prayer

Mountain. When she lost her appetite and lost weight, he insisted.

Finally, Chongja agreed and went with her husband to Prayer Mountain for three days. Chongja was so weak already that she could not fast; so her husband prayed and fasted on her behalf. Then, the second day they were there—surrounded by prayer and challenged by faith-provoking sermons—Chongja's heart softened. For the first time in many months, Chongja cried out to God. She asked God to forgive her greed in buying the lottery ticket and to forgive her for letting her heart become hard toward Him.

"I repented of all the sins I could think of," Chongja said, "and then asked God to heal me. I told Him that if He did not heal me, I could not continue living. When I rebuked what Satan was doing in my life, I quoted Luke 10:19, 'I have given you authority to trample on snakes and scorpions and to overcome all the power of the enemy; nothing will harm you.' Suddenly I felt like something was loosed from my head, and a wave of refreshing flowed through me. I knew then I was healed, and began thanking God."

After her time at Prayer Mountain, a different Chongja started attending church again, even going to Friday all-night prayer meetings with her husband. It wasn't long before a peaceful and calm Chongja became pregnant and gave birth to a baby boy. Chongja and her husband now serve as layleaders in the church.

Is everyone who goes to Prayer Mountain healed? No, One staff pastor added, "But most who have been healed have been persistent, sometimes coming to Prayer Mountain on several occasions to pray and fast."

4

The Ministry of Layleaders

In October 1961, with the name Full Gospel Revival Center, the pastoral staff moved their crusade meetings from a tent to a newly built, prefabricated building. Praying to attract an increasing crowd, they invited various speakers. Dad remembers: "There was a definite move of God during those meetings. Hundreds were born again, dozens were physically healed, and many were baptized in the Holy Spirit and spoke in tongues. By the time we completed the 1,500-seat sanctuary, nearly five hundred people met with us for regular worship services."

A Lay Leadership Structure

After a few months, many of the regular attendees pressed the staff to make the revival center a genuine church. Not only that, the young Cho informed Dad, "I want to appoint deacons and deaconesses."

"I was hesitant," says my dad. "My background had been different. On occasion, American church deacon boards became power platforms to command pastors and congregations to do their bidding. Some of the deacons I knew had a keen business sense but little true spirituality. Problems resulted."

So Cho asked Dad to come to a meeting with their growing group of layworkers. Dad watched as Cho taught them about servanthood, thanked them for their faithfulness in ministry, and encouraged them to continue ministering to others.

Dad related, "Those gathered were the men and women who faithfully helped in ushering and controlling the crowd during services, who taught the children and youth, and who spent untold hours visiting the homes of recent converts and the sick. As I sat there thinking, I saw a different perspective. These were the people Yonggi Cho wanted to appoint as deacons and deaconesses—faithful individuals active in ministry to others, unlike some of the deacons I had known. Sitting in the midst of that faithful ministering group, I became convinced."

On May 13, 1962, the church officially changed their name to Full Gospel Central Church and, not long after, they appointed deacons and deaconesses. In my father's words, "Rather than have a parade of evangelists and speakers to attract a crowd, we focused on teaching and motivating believers to minister and reach out to others. For that to take place, there had to be a structure of layleaders. The growing crowd soon became a vibrant congregation."

One woman's statement summed up the attitude of these layleaders: "Before I became a deaconess, I worked for the church mainly to help my pastor. I enjoyed visiting homes, ministering to people, and helping prepare monthly Communion. But after I became a deaconess, my perspective changed. I no longer worked from duty. My service became my assignment from heaven. I realized then that I was serving God."

YFGC openly recognizes and encourages its layleaders. The church holds semiannual seminars for the cell group leaders—the largest group of layleaders—to thank them for past service and to motivate them in the tasks ahead. Dr. Cho interweaves testimonies and accounts of layleaders throughout many of his sermons, showing the importance and effectiveness of layministry.

A Priority of Ministry

The first principle that guides the actions of YFGC is that top priority must be given to evangelism. Layleaders consider evangelism paramount. "When Jesus said to 'go out and preach the gospel,'" one layleader emphasized, "He wasn't talking to someone else. He was talking to you and me."

Most men's groups meet in homes; Heechong Lee's group,

however, meets during the work week in his office, for it is composed of his company's seventeen employees, many of whom were not Christians when such meetings began.

"We use the text and format given by the church," Heechong explained. "We rotate the roles of presider and prayer captain among all who attend—including the non-Christians. At first I made the meeting mandatory for my employees, but they did not respond well. So then I made participation voluntary, and most still came. More than ten of my employees have become genuine Christians."

A retired fifty-nine-year-old widow, Yunhyung Yu is among YFGC's faithful layleaders who take Jesus' command to reach others seriously. After Yunhyung became a Christian, she attended every church and cell meeting possible, helping others in any way she could. After only two years, the church appointed her as a deaconess and home cell leader. During the three years she was a cell leader, this gentle, soft-spoken woman led fifty people to a saving relationship with Jesus Christ, as well as directed them to involvement in the church.

For the next four and one-half years, Yunhyung served as a section leader, overseeing eight cell groups in the Sodaemoon area. "The most important principles I learned as a section leader," Yunhyung said, "were watchfulness and persistence. The cell leader is to be watchful for receptive unbelievers in his or her community, and bring them to church. There were many Sundays I went to church three and four times, each time with a different unbeliever."

A Caring Network of Ministering Believers

Layleaders maintain a constant posture of ministry and often visit others in their homes. On a typical day Yunhyung Yu spends six to seven hours visiting and ministering in an average of ten homes, including the homes of her cell leaders and their cell members.

"My primary responsibility," she said, "is to oversee and minister to my cell leaders. I am always checking to see if they are following through and caring for their cell group members. Some of the believers they work with are poor and struggle a great deal. So it is vital that we pray and continually encourage them with the Word of God."

Yunhyung added, "It is also crucial to be persistent with the new convert. I remember six believers in our section, each of whom had dropped out of church and a cell group. We began visiting them weekly, encouraging each one in the Christian walk. In every case, it was not too long until they began attending church and their home cell meetings again."

This posture of ministry, often reflected in home visitation, is not limited to women. Daegyu Park is a senior deacon who volunteers his Sunday afternoons in the Men's Visitation Office at the church's World Mission Center.

Deacon Park explained, "The most important function of the senior deacon is home visitation. Most senior deacons sit together in a designated section of the church during the nine o'clock Sunday morning worship service. We then come to this large room for a special service just for senior deacons. After that, we divide into teams of three and four and visit the men and men's cell leaders of the congregation. So many are salaried employees of companies that Sunday afternoon is the only time we can visit them in their homes."

Layleaders like Daegyu Park and Yunhyung Yu have created a caring network of ministering believers. They serve as living examples of Paul's instruction that a deacon be "worthy of respect, sincere . . . keep[ing] hold of the deep truths of the faith with a clear conscience" (1 Timothy 3:8–9).

Some in YFGC speak of two channels of ministry in this caring network. One is ministry to the church, through such avenues as singing in one of the twelve adult choirs, ushering, and preparing monthly Communion. The second is ministry to the community, primarily through home visitation and leadership of a neighborhood cell group, caring for church members as well as unbelievers in that community.

Many YFGC layleaders become involved in both avenues of ministry. "But," one deacon related, "I enjoy home visitation and my cell group more. As you Americans say, 'That's where the action is.'"

The Responsibility of Prayer

Prayer is vital to each layleader. Changki Song, professor of Chinese literature in a Korean university, was a men's cell group leader for many years before becoming an elder. He said, "The teaching in my group focused on daily Christian living. But the primary thing we did in my group was pray. There are so many needs: family problems, health, the difficulties of human relationships. The most prevalent problem I found relates to one's job situation—getting a good job, earning enough money to make ends meet. I have seen God meet the needs of many people."

He continued, "If I were to give advice to a new group leader, it would be this: Your group might be small, but your responsibility is noble and serious. You must be certain to pray every day. Pray daily for your members, not just for yourself. To pray for another is better than praying for oneself."

As leadership responsibility increases so does the importance of prayer. The higher a person is in leadership, the more time that person is to spend in prayer.

Appointment of Layleaders

Most layleaders have been born again through the ministry of others in the church.[1] Such was the case of Heechong Lee. Before he became a believer, his wife grew ill after giving birth to their second child. During the next eighteen months, she was hospitalized three times. Her five-foot three-inch frame shrank to seventy pounds, in spite of the medications doctors tried. One of the couple's neighbors was the leader of a neighborhood women's cell group and asked Heechong's wife to go to church with her. Although Heechong had been raised in a Buddhist family, by that point he was willing for his wife to try anything. So she went with the cell leader to a worship service at YFGC.

Heechong waited for his wife to return. When she went to the service that day, she gave her life to Jesus Christ. "How well I remember the big smile on her face when she came back," Heechong said. "My wife had not been smiling much through her illness. That big smile on her face really impressed me. It made me curious to know what had changed her."

His wife accompanied the cell leader to Prayer Mountain, where they prayed and fasted three days for her healing. The next month, Dr. Cho prayed for her, and she instantly felt a warmth surge from her head to her feet. Ten days later, she threw her medicine away. In a short time, the healed woman worried about gaining too much weight.

YFGC's layleaders recruit new converts, minister to them, and pray with them. The new convert often responds by joining the church and, if faithful, later becomes a deacon. This was the pattern for Heechong, who decided to join his wife, accepted Jesus as his Savior, and then registered as a member of the church. After two years, Heechong was made a deacon, and within a year and a half the church appointed him as a men's home cell leader.

YFGC first looks for a believer's faithfulness before appointing him as a layleader. The church recognizes that not all are equally gifted in ministry but that everyone can be faithful. YFGC teaches that one shows faithfulness in response to small things—prompt attendance at church and cell meetings, acts of kindness to others, persistence in prayer and sharing the gospel. Jesus said, "He that is faithful in that which is least is faithful also in much" (Luke 16:10). In the Parable of the Talents, Jesus pointed to God's view of faithfulness in the master's response to his servants. To two of his servants he said, "Well done, good and faithful servant! You have been faithful with a few things; I will put you in charge of many things" (Matthew 25:21; see also v. 23).

This same principle is applied by Paul (1 Timothy 3:10): "They must first be tested; and then if there is nothing against them, let them serve as deacons." Once a year, usually by October, the pastoral staff gives written nominations recommending potential deacons and deaconesses, senior deacons and deaconesses, and elders. The appropriate pastors and elders approve the written nominations and submit them to the church's Pastoral Care Department, which reviews each person's information and confirms that the person qualifies. Dr. Cho gives final appointment, with a certificate of appointment sealed with his *tojan*, the Korean seal indicating formal personal approval. Official appointment is made public in a special service, often held the following June.

The selection process for home cell leaders and section leaders is much the same. However, the need for cell group and section leaders is more ongoing. Their public presentation is usually made in front of their peers in their area's monthly section meeting, held in a neighborhood home.

The Ladder of Leadership

Throughout the years there has been an average of one layleader to every ten to sixteen church members.[2] As the congregation increased, so did the levels of layleadership. Besides deacons and deaconesses, faithful deacons became senior deacons and, later, elders. Faithful deaconesses became senior deaconesses.[3]

YFGC keeps a focus on faithfulness throughout what some have termed YFGC's ladder of leadership.

Elders
Senior Deacons and Deaconesses
Section Leaders
Cell Group Leaders
Deacons and Deaconesses

DEACONS AND DEACONESSES

The first rung on this ladder of leadership is appointment as a deacon or deaconess. To be a deacon or deaconess, one must have been a faithful member of the church for at least two years, have been baptized in water, and have a consistent record of giving. He or she is to be a good Christian example, with no outstanding financial or personal problems with others, and a faithful participant in a cell group. He or she is to be at least thirty years of age if married or thirty-five if single.

According to Kangman Lee, a deacon in the church's Pastoral Care Department, about 70 percent of the deacons and deaconesses serve solely as cell leaders. The remaining 30 percent also serves in other ways, such as ushering or crowd control during, before, and after worship services. During the services, when the congregation sings together, they are not led by a staff pastor but by one of several senior deacons who stands at the pulpit on the church's lower platform. Certain senior deacons and senior deaconesses wearing the Korean national dress collect the offering.

The title of deacon or deaconess is given indefinitely or until that individual is promoted to a higher level of responsibility.[4] Most aspire to greater responsibility and service to God, a desire some have dubbed "holy ambition." (See also Appendix 2: Deacons in One Church in America.)

The Women's Fellowship

The Women's Fellowship was started in 1960 to support church ministries. Although not all deaconesses are involved with the Women's Fellowship, the nearly four thousand that are belong to one of seven divisions and do most of their work on Sunday.

More than a hundred workers in the Communion Division prepare the monthly Communion elements, annually using more than sixty-five thousand pounds of grapes and seventy thousand pounds of sugar just for the juice. Members of the Evangelism Division visit the sick in hospitals, do street evangelism, distribute Christian literature, and support the military outreach and home missionaries. The General Affairs Division arranges special support for church events—even helping to serve pastors and employees in the church cafeteria. Those in the Planning Division schedule the annual interdenominational Women's Fasting Conference at Prayer Mountain, provide music for certain events, and arrange and decorate room facilities. Deaconesses in the Ceremony Division help with weddings and funerals, often accompanying pastors to give congratulations or condolences.

The largest division is the Service Division. More than four hundred deaconesses from this division join deacons to rotate services and serve as greeters, ushers, and to collect offerings. Others help new converts prepare for water baptism, serve as receptionists for pastors' seminars, and even prepare the robes to be worn by the adult choirs.

Large wooden boxes monitored by deaconesses of the Rice Tithe Division are stationed around the main church campus. Some believers still tithe rice. Many cell groups collect rice to bring to the collection points on Sundays. Near certain rice boxes are bins for the collection of used clothing. During the week the church distributes rice and clothing to the poor and needy, pioneer churches, and seminary and Bible school students.

One Sunday between services, I stood watching near a rice tithe collection bin. A woman came up to the bin clutching a bag of rice in her hands. The deaconess overseeing the bin placed her hands on the bag, and both women bowed their heads in prayer. For the next two minutes the deaconess prayed, thanking God for the rice and blessing the woman who gave, asking God to give her a return of thirty, sixty, or a hundred times. Then the deaconess lovingly poured the rice through a slot into the bin. The other woman smiled, took her empty bag, and disappeared into the crowd. Then someone else came up, and the entire process was repeated. By Sunday evening, the large bin was full.

The Men's Fellowship

The Men's Fellowship was started in 1968 to cultivate fellowship among the men and to render service to the church. It has a current membership of more than sixty-five hundred, primarily deacons.

"We feel there are three areas of importance for our members," explained Elder Soontae Kim, former vice president of the fellowship. "First, our members must study the Word of God. Second, we encourage our members to receive the baptism in the Holy Spirit and live prayerful, Spirit-filled lives. Third, our members should participate fully in church life and be active in some type of continuing involvement." Once a person becomes a layleader, he or she also will become more visible to the congregation. More than a thousand deacons are involved in ushering, collecting offerings, and crowd control. Each Saturday and Sunday worship service, more than ninety deacons from the Men's Fellowship and seventy deaconesses from the Women's Fellowship stand at main entrances and greet, including giving out a copy of the bulletin, and usher people. Some guide foreign visitors to a special section in the balcony where they can hear certain services translated into English, Japanese, Mandarin, and other languages through earphones. Other deacons and deaconesses stand at central points in the sanctuary and over-flow chapels to offer help in finding an empty seat or to assist if any problems arise. Others outside in the parking lots and road-ways help in directing traffic.

That same worship service requires that sixty deacons scatter onto the parking lots and sidewalks to help with traffic, as well as crowd control. Primarily because of the organizational ability of the Men's Fellowship, the traffic runs smoothly, and people enter and leave the services rapidly.

One deacon from the Men's Fellowship declared, "Sunday is a long day for me. I start at seven-thirty with a morning worship and devotional service in the Men's Fellowship office and usher in services until nine that night. Some deacons do this only once a month, but I choose to serve almost every Sunday. And why not? Jesus Christ forgave my sins and gave me new life. I find great pleasure in working for my Lord this way."

One division of the Men's Fellowship, consisting of senior dea-cons, counts the offerings, which are taken to a nearby bank each Sunday. Another division handles the hundreds of new con-verts' blue decision cards put in the offering bags. They record the information on the cards in a ledger, sort the cards by geo-graphical district, then hand deliver them to the appropriate district office for follow-up. Men's Fellowship members complete a white visitation slip on each male convert, then put it in the slot of the male cell leader nearest the convert's home. The home cell leader visits that new convert as soon as possible—usually the same week—welcoming him to the upcoming weekly cell group meeting in his neighborhood.

Yet another division of the Men's Fellowship concerns itself with outreach and oversees the men's cell groups. A major por-tion of the fellowship's huge office is taken up by more than twenty desks, each used for reporting and transferring informa-tion for the men's cell group leaders in specific geographical areas. Each male cell leader visits the office on Sunday to turn in the offering from his last cell meeting and to pick up the names and information on any new converts in his area.

Cell Group Leaders

Once someone is appointed to the post of deacon or deaconess, he or she is considered a potential home cell group leader, the second rung on the ladder of leadership.[5] Dynamic home cell groups require good leaders. As one member said, "A good group starts with a good leader. A good cell group meeting starts with a leader who is prayerfully prepared."

According to Taeho Kim, a male cell leader, it is necessary that cell group leaders have a vibrant daily personal relationship with Jesus Christ. "I have observed," said Taeho, "that if a leader himself has had a definite experience with God and His power to transform lives, then his own faith grows. If his own faith grows, he is then more evangelistic and full of faith to others. The transforming power of the baptism of the Holy Spirit still astounds me."

The Korean name for a group leader is *ku-yok jang*, which means "leader in one's small geographical territory or area." Group leaders do more than have a weekly meeting; they have spiritual oversight of a specified area and are responsible to visit participants and reach out to non-Christian neighbors. One cell leader shared her personal monthly calendar with me. Each week she had a four-hour segment for home visitation—two hours to group members and two hours to non-Christians in her community. "On that day," she explained, "I make breakfast for my family before they leave for work and school, and then I make home ministry visits. The first two hours I visit our newest members or those in difficulty. The next two hours I go to every home in our community to distribute copies of the weekly church newspaper. By the time my children return from school, I'm back home, encouraged by the most blessed four hours of my week."

As the group grows, an assistant is chosen and the group often splits in two—like some living cells—to form two groups. Because of this, foreigners call them "cell groups" and their leadership "cell group leaders."

Church leaders spot most potential group leaders within existing groups. One subdistrict pastor told me, "Once I see a person I consider a potential leader, I tell the area section layleader to watch that person for six months. If he proves faithful in church and cell attendance and shows fervency in his Christian walk, he will probably be selected as an assistant cell leader."

Characteristics of Potential Leaders

In talking with YFGC staff pastors, I discovered five characteristics they commonly look for in potential leaders.[6]

CONTAGIOUS ENTHUSIASM

Staff pastors first look for believers who are enthusiastic in witnessing and in their Christian walk and have a positive attitude about divine intervention in human problems. One staff pastor told me, "When a person has a problem, he does not need human sympathy. He does need someone to join with him in faith-filled prayer and point him to Jesus Christ, the Master Problem Solver."

CLEAR TESTIMONY

An effective testimony is not only enthusiastic but also clear, direct, and specific. Leaders who have personally experienced the power of God in healing, deliverance, or miracles are best able to communicate the power and goodness of God to others. One member explained, "Once a person has had a definite, specific experience of the power of God, how can he be anything else but effective in evangelism? All that person needs to do is tell others what God has already done in his life."

However, not all groups or leaders are equally evangelistic. One staff pastor reported that some leaders are just good Christians who take care of fellow believers. But the evangelistic cell leader usually has had personal experience of God's power in his life and is eager to share that with others.

DEDICATION

The potential cell leader must also be dedicated to God, biblical truth and principle, and church leadership. This dedication is reflected in faithfully attending church and home cell meetings and in continued submission to authority. In the words of one staff pastor, "You can help a person increase his ability, but you can't make him faithful and dedicated. I first look for someone who has the character quality of faithfulness, then help him with his abilities."

It is also felt that leaders should consistently tithe. Some staff pastors refer to the principle in Matthew 6:21—"Where your treasure is, there your heart will be also." According to an older staff pastor, "If a person cannot trust God with 10 percent of his money, how can God trust him with the leadership of His children?"

ACCESS TO TIME AND MONEY

Cell leaders need time to minister to others—both during and between group meetings. They need time to prepare, time to hold a weekly meeting, and time to make weekly home ministry visits. They also need money to help others and to contribute at the weddings, birthdays, and other significant events in the lives of their cell members and families.

SPIRIT-LED LIFE

Most importantly, staff pastors look for potential leaders who are filled with the Holy Spirit and are sensitive to God's guidance in their daily lives. Not all cell leaders have received the baptism in the Holy Spirit, but all are to be persistent in praying for others, never giving up until God has spoken. "The most evangelistic leaders I have known," said a prominent staff pastor, "are continually filled with the Holy Spirit. Only through God's Holy Spirit can we be motivated to pray persistently."

A large portion of the Spirit-led life involves being a person of prayer. According to Dongho Kim, a senior deacon who has worked several years with the church's cell groups, "The prayer life of the cell leader is of utmost importance. The effective cell leader is diligent and fervent in Bible study, home visitation, and evangelism. But prayer is the most important element in the life of the effective home cell leader."

Once staff pastors spot potential leaders and talk to cell and section leaders, they submit their names to elders and more senior pastors in the area, so that no significant facts about that person will be overlooked.[7] Once approved, each new home cell leader receives an official certificate of appointment signed by Dr. Cho, the current study guide for that year, an annual pocket handbook, and an official attaché case with the church emblem on the outside. These cases serve as the cell leader's public badge of identification. Most leaders use them to carry their Bibles, hymnbooks, note pads, and study guides. Seasoned cell leaders have been known to brag, "I made so many home visits to my people that I wore out my attaché and had to get a new one."

Training Cell Group Leaders

YFGC gives new cell group leaders both initial and ongoing training.[8] YFGC's Education Division coordinates initial leadership training through the eight-week Cell Leaders' College.[9] Personnel and district pastors teach two subjects in each of these Sunday afternoon classes, held in one of YFGC's smaller auditoriums.

Limited ongoing training occurs during the semiannual Section Leaders'/Cell Leaders' Conference, held once in the spring and once in the fall. In years past, each conference was three days long and included inspirational messages, practical tips, and new worship songs; but in recent years, because the number of cell group leaders has grown, YFGC shortened the conferences to a single meeting, with an informative lecture and a challenging message from Dr. Cho. Even so, the number of cell leaders requires that the meeting be repeated the next day; that is, half the cell leaders come one day and the other half the next—packing the sanctuary both times.

Most ongoing leadership training occurs as section leaders spend time with group leaders, both during ministry visits and during group meetings. One survey showed that a little more than half the current cell leaders first served as assistant leaders.[10] Some of them did not even go through the Cell Leaders' College.

SECTION LEADERS

After effectively serving two years as a cell group leader, the layleader is eligible to become a section leader, often overseeing between three and eight cell group leaders. Section layleaders are key people (the "middle management" of the cell system— see Appendix 3: Three Kinds of Group Systems), being a vital link between busy staff pastors and the cell leaders. "I believe," said one staff pastor, "that the section leader is the most important member of the church. By the time a person becomes a section leader, it is vital that he or she be baptized in the Holy Spirit and speak in tongues. Only then can he or she be properly empowered in service."

Staff Pastor Leebu Pak relates her approach to selecting a section leader. She looks at all the cell leaders in a geographical section and nominates the one who has done the most evangelism. Then she evaluates that person's faithfulness.

Another staff pastor added, "Before nominating someone as a section leader, I also look at his or her financial status. A section leader must have the financial resources to give at weddings, funerals, and other important occasions. Also, since a meeting with all the leaders of that section will be held in the section leader's home each month, it is important that the section leader own his or her own home. It is vital that the section leader be knowledgeable about life, have strong faith, and be well-educated and intelligent. We don't want someone perfect, but the section leader must be spiritually and emotionally mature."

One responsibility of section leaders is the ongoing training of cell group leaders. They do this most often by modeling, especially as they go with cell leaders in ministry visits. In addition, there is a monthly leaders' meeting in each section, when the group leaders of that area meet with their staff pastor in the home of the section leader for prayer and ministry. After this meeting, the staff pastor usually goes with the section leader and group leaders to make ministry visits to the homes and businesses of those in that area undergoing the most difficulty. As the staff pastor ministers and prays with these people, section and group leaders are often writing notes and learning by observing.

Many staff pastors consider home visitation to struggling members the most important responsibility of the section leader. Some section leaders talk to all their home cell leaders on the phone every day, others at least once a week. A section leader then takes a portion of one day a week to visit the cell leaders and members who are having the most difficulty or struggle.

One section leader explained, "I meet with my seven cell leaders in my home every Thursday. We sing together, pray together, and then discuss the upcoming cell lesson. We talk about any problems and how they can be solved. Then we pray again. If any cell leader is particularly having difficulty, I will spend more time with her. I then try to go to various cell meetings, especially those with problems, and help any way I can."

SENIOR DEACONS AND DEACONESSES

When a deacon has faithfully served five years, usually as a home cell group leader, he is eligible to be nominated and appointed as a senior deacon.[11] Becoming a senior deacon—more accurately translated, "anointed deacon"—is an especially sacred appointment. His public presentation is official after an ordained pastor lays hands on him, prays, and anoints him for special service.

"In reality," said one man, "the senior deacon is in preparation to become an elder."

One senior deacon said, "Let me put it this way. If the church is like an army, the senior deacons are the sergeants and the elders are the officers."

Kwansa is the highest title a laywoman can have. Some translate *kwansa* "senior deaconess," and perceive it as the counterpart of senior deacon. Others translate *kwansa* "female elder." These female spiritual prayer warriors are a caring network who support the elders and pastors through their active daily prayer and intercession.[12]

In any case, a key function of the senior deaconess is to accompany her staff pastor on visitation, especially when the staff pastor is male. Staff pastors utilize senior deaconesses in two primary ways. Some staff pastors have four or five senior deaconesses who take turns going on visitation with them during different days of the week. In a growing trend, others have put each senior deaconess over a specific number of section leaders, taking the senior deaconess whenever he visits members of her sections.

When discussing the role of YFGC's senior deaconesses, all agree that these older women are the nurturing spiritual mothers in the church and form the congregation's "prayer backbone."

The Senior Deaconesses' Fellowship

Senior deaconesses who desire to do so can be members of the Senior Deaconesses' Fellowship. During the week, these older women focus on daily prayer and intercession, as well as visitation, often with a staff pastor.

Their activities are not limited to prayer and ministry visits. Explained one senior deaconess, "We also help finance the broadcasting of Dr. Cho's program on the domestic television station in Ulsan, send financial aid to indigent Korean Bible school students, and help start Korean churches in areas where there is not yet a church."

Each Sunday morning at eleven o'clock, senior deaconesses join for a special hour of prayer in a spacious room designated for the Senior Deaconesses' Fellowship. Any urgent matters for prayer become their focus, and they all pray aloud for God to break through in particular situations. "We always receive an answer when we pray in this way," Senior Deaconess Oaksohn Kim said.

One senior deaconess told of an incident when there was sharp disagreement among some leaders in the church over a particular issue. "Without going into unnecessary detail," the senior deaconess said, "we prayed for this in our service. The following week, those leaders came to an agreement. The unity and sense of partnership in our church were restored."

"Most senior deaconesses," she added, "spend two hours in prayer every day—for their families, for our country, and especially for Dr. Cho, the leaders of the church, and those they visit in their homes."

The Senior Deacons' Fellowship

The Senior Deacons' Fellowship also has its weekly service Sunday mornings at eleven, in a separate room from the deaconesses. Many of the church's senior deacons belong to this fellowship, serving as section leaders of men's cell groups, directors in various children's Sunday school departments, spiritual life leaders in the choirs, and participants in the outreach fellowships.

Each Sunday afternoon, at least a hundred senior deacons go

to the Men's Home Visitation Office to pray and divide into teams for visitation. Each team makes five visits, usually to the homes of cell group leaders who have become discouraged.

Fred Rodriguez, an Assemblies of God pastor in Lake Elsinore, California, accompanied one team from the Senior Deacons' Fellowship to a cell leader's home. Pastor Rodriguez said, "This cell leader worked in a metalwork factory where there had been several accidents. One man had cut off his finger. This cell leader was concerned for his safety and that of his coworkers. The four men on the visitation team prayed with him, read Scripture to him, and encouraged him. They told him they would continue to pray for God to intervene on his behalf, and that God would keep him and his coworkers safe at work. What impressed me most was the sincere concern they expressed to him and the depth of ministry that took place that Sunday afternoon."

ELDERS

Elder is the highest title a layman at YFGC can hold. Many elders often serve as laypreachers in their neighborhood men's groups and at certain ministry functions.[13] The church gives elders gold pins of identification, which they wear on their suit lapel each time they go to a service. Elders wear white gloves the first Sunday of every month when they distribute the Communion elements. A different elder prays in each worship service, always certain to include the church's layleaders in his petition to God.

According to Elder Sokho Kim, elders are "to visit the sick in their homes, give advice and counsel to laymen, and form the advising body to Dr. Cho in his decision-making for matters related to the advancement of the church."

Dr. Cho explains the role of elders this way: "Pastors, deacons, and deaconesses are in charge of ministry to people. Elders assist me in the important responsibility of conducting the business matters of the church.[14] The elders also oversee and advise me in setting the church's business and administrative policy. This frees the hands of the pastors, deacons, and deaconesses to focus on ministry."

Each year, the church holds three joint sessions of all the

elders and some of the ordained pastors. One of these sessions focuses on the proposed budget for the upcoming year.[15] At the end of the year, usually in December, another joint session meets to evaluate the budget from the previous year. This system frees Dr. Cho and the pastoral staff from any taint of financial mishandling.

In the words of one visiting American minister, "A setup like this has built-in checks and balances. It was interesting to me that many of those elders were born again under Dr. Cho's ministry and then began to serve in the church. There is potential for conflict, yet there is harmony. I understand now why the members of the congregation trust their church."

YFGC's layleaders not only trust their church, they also spend thousands of hours each week in both prayer and ministry.

5

Home Cell Groups

In its earlier years, YFGC was much more traditional in its approach: Home groups were not a consideration. Lay involvement was limited primarily to home visitation and the activities needed for smooth-flowing church services. Then one undesired crisis led to a transition that changed both YFGC's future and its growth pattern.

In 1964, the church, then at Sodaemoon, had been growing, soon to reach the three thousand mark. Most layleaders served as children's Sunday school teachers, as choir members in one of the church's two choirs, as Women's Fellowship helpers, or as ushers. Some women layleaders worked with Jashil Choi and formed teams active in home visitation. It was an exciting church with a fairly traditional structure.

Dr. Cho had taken his role as senior pastor quite seriously. He preached the two Sunday morning services, the Wednesday evening service, and nearly every early morning prayer meeting. When there was a wedding or funeral to be performed, he would officiate. When there was a home to be visited, he would go. When someone came to the office for counseling, he would pray with him. He felt the responsibility of doing everything himself. After all, he was the senior pastor, and God did work mightily through him.

The Turning Point of Crisis

One summer Sunday, Dr. Cho preached the two morning services. As always he preached well, but there was a tired and worn look about him.

That afternoon he was to baptize three hundred new converts, since the weather was warm.[1] My concerned father offered to help.

"No," Dr. Cho protested. "I'm all right. I'm strong. Besides, it's my responsibility."

So three hundred times Dr. Cho lowered bodies into the water, baptizing them "in the name of the Father, the Son, and the Holy Spirit."

Later that afternoon, Dr. Cho was to go to the airport to meet a visiting American evangelist and interpret for him during the evening service. Again, Dad offered to help, saying, "I can meet him at the airport for you. You get some rest."

Again Dr. Cho refused, "No. He's expecting me."

So Dr. Cho went to the airport, took the visiting evangelist to the hotel, and went to church for the evening service. He had not even had a chance to eat.

When the evening service started, Dad sat in a chair on the platform. As missionary advisor, Dad usually spoke on Sunday evenings;[2] and when there were guest speakers he was there to help.

I sat beside my mother in our usual pew, listening as the choir sang. When it was time for the sermon, Dr. Cho walked slowly to the pulpit and stood shakily to the left of the evangelist. For a few minutes, everything seemed fine. Dr. Cho interpreted each phrase of the fiery minister's sermons, even trying to gesture and move the same way the speaker did. Then Cho's legs began to quiver. Suddenly, he collapsed and dropped to the floor, his lean body limp on the wooden platform.

Dad rushed from his chair and knelt at Dr. Cho's side. "John," he faintly called to Dad, "I'm dying."

Deacons of the church quickly arranged to rush Dr. Cho by stretcher to a nearby hospital. I went with Dad and Mom, and we followed closely behind, leaving a startled guest evangelist with a different interpreter to preach to a now somber congregation. I stayed near my parents and other believers. Most sat with heads bowed, praying for God to heal their young pastor.

A doctor finally came to examine Dr. Cho's still body. The doctor spent several minutes looking over reports of the tests. Then he turned to us: "This man is physically exhausted. His health has been broken, and his heart is weak. To recover, he will require total bed rest." The doctor paused, then continued, "After that, it would be my suggestion that he find another line of work. It would be better if he never preached or pastored again. The strain could kill him."

Dr. Cho would need all the rest he could get. This crisis needed a quick solution. Temporarily, Dad and Jashil Choi divided the pastoral duties between them.

"Church in the Home"

During his weeks of recuperation, Dr. Cho had limited participation in church services. Most of the time he spent in bed—praying, resting, and reading his Bible.

Dr. Cho knew he could no longer shoulder the burden of the entire church. Yes, the church had been effective. But he knew it would be physically impossible for him to continue in the same way.

So he read the Bible, searching for solutions. As he read the Book of Acts, he noted the growth and ministry pattern in the Early Church. On the Day of Pentecost three thousand people accepted Jesus Christ. In Acts 4, the number had grown to five thousand. By chapter 5, multitudes were coming to Christ. And the Holy Spirit added to their number daily.

Those believers went to synagogues or the temple but did not have a single large gathering place. And those multitudes of believers had only nineteen leaders: twelve apostles and seven deacons. Dr. Cho wondered how the Early Church in Jerusalem cared for such large numbers. He couldn't even care adequately for his congregation of three thousand.

Dr. Cho read again and noted that the Christians met from "house to house," breaking bread and sharing apostolic doctrine (Acts 2:42–46). Those thousands of believers broke into home meetings. Not only did they visit homes, but they also held worship services in homes. Later, Priscilla and Aquila held church services in their home, as did Nympha and Philemon and his family (see Romans 16:3–5; 1 Corinthians 16:19; Colossians 4:15; Philemon 1–2).

Even when Dr. Cho's congregation had met under the tent,

they had divided the community into four areas. They appointed a contact person for each area, and sometimes held services in the different areas. But the pattern from Acts seemed even more aggressive.

Cho also read parts of the Old Testament and was struck by the story in Exodus 18:13–26. The scenario of this passage was clear: Moses was overworked by hearing the problems of all the people who gathered before him each day. His father-in-law, Jethro, could see that Moses would soon wear himself out.

As Dr. Cho identified with Moses, Jethro's advice was clear: "Select capable men from all the people—men who fear God, trustworthy men who hate dishonest gain—and appoint them as officials over thousands, hundreds, fifties and tens. . . . That will make your load lighter, because they will share it with you. If you do this, and God so commands, you will be able to stand the strain, and all these people will go home satisfied" (Exodus 18:21–23).

When Dr. Cho prayed, his mandate seemed firm: He was to use his deacons as leaders of home services—the biblical "church in the home"—to meet during the week throughout the city. Dr. Cho would preach the Sunday morning and Wednesday evening worship services. It seemed such a wonderful, biblical plan. Dr. Cho shared it with Dad and Jashil Choi; all were in agreement.

Introducing the New Concept

Dr. Cho finally gathered enough strength to go to a meeting of his deacons and male layleaders. He shared with them how God had been dealing with him about appointing layleaders to have home meetings. But they were not receptive to the idea.

One deacon stated that he was too tired at the end of the day to lead a meeting. Another insisted that some groups would get proud, break away, and start their own churches. A third layleader remarked that it sounded biblical, but they had not been trained for anything like this. This plan was not part of traditional church activity. "Besides," he informed Dr. Cho, "that's what we pay you for." The meeting ended with the leaders' suggestion: "Why don't you get away and take a long vacation?"

Dr. Cho returned home discouraged. His first attempt at getting home groups started was unsuccessful. Traditional thinking was too strong among his male layleaders.

Jashil Choi often joined with a group of women who had been effective in making home ministry visits, which frequently resulted in spontaneous home meetings. They talked to Dr. Cho about using women as home group leaders, but he was reluctant. Women in the Korean culture were considered inferior to men and were not valued for their leadership potential; however, since most were homemakers, they had access to a valuable commodity: time to care and minister to others. The Korean cultural bias favoring men, as well as certain Scripture passages, added to his hesitancy; nevertheless, as he studied the Bible, his own objections lessened. When Cho prayed, he was reminded by the Lord how often He had used women in ministry, and sensed this dialogue:

"Who gave birth to Jesus?"

"Mary, a woman," Dr. Cho responded.

"Who nurtured Jesus?" came a second question.

"Mary, a woman," Dr. Cho responded a second time.

"Who surrounded Jesus' ministry and supplied His needs?" came a third question.

"A group of women," was Dr. Cho's reply.

"Who remained until the last moment of His passion on the cross?"

"Women."

"Who came on the first day of Jesus' resurrection, and saw His empty tomb?"

"Women."

"To whom did Christ first speak so the message of His resurrection would be given to the apostles?"

"A woman."

So Dr. Cho turned to the deaconesses in the Women's Fellowship. When he spoke to them about his physical weakness, several cried. When he explained that the only way he could continue pastoring was to follow the biblical pattern of layleaders having home meetings throughout the city, they listened with interest. Then they responded, "Tell us to do anything and we will obey. We will do the work."

When Dr. Cho announced to the deacons that he was going to

use women as group leaders, they balked. Some banded together and stated that they would leave the church if women were used. He responded to the disgruntled deacons, "All right, if that is what you have decided, go ahead and leave. When I asked you deacons to have home meetings, you refused. But I am still sick, and I have no alternative. I feel like God has cornered me in this situation and left me no other choice. I have to use the women."

The First Home Cell Groups

The first home cell groups soon formed. Since Dr. Cho still struggled with chronic weakness, Jashil Choi took charge of organization. Twenty women in different areas throughout the city were selected as the first leaders.

Only two guidelines were given. First, each leader was to gather and care for the believing Christians in her area, teaching the Bible and praying together. Second, each leader was to go out and win her neighbors to Jesus Christ, then invite them to her home meetings and to church.

Each leader could choose what she wanted to share in the group. Some played audiocassettes; others invited outside speakers to share. Those first groups were attended primarily by other women, with twenty to thirty in each group.

Even though Dr. Cho had clearly explained to the congregation how God was leading him, only a portion of the congregation participated. The response was disappointing; even so, Dr. Cho knew God had spoken to him. For a time, things seemed to go fairly well.

However, problems soon surfaced. A new Christian in one group asked the leader what the word *trinity* meant. The ignorant but sincere leader stated, "Well, I think it means our God has one body but three heads."

Other leaders invited to their group meetings speakers who taught a different theological position from the church. As a result, one man came into a group and stopped the meeting. Another man became so upset about his wife leading a group and praying for people that he hit her.

With few exceptions, those first groups collapsed. Several men in the church were pleased.

Yet, when Dr. Cho turned to the Lord in prayer, God encouraged him to persist despite the problems.

Another Attempt at Home Cell Groups

When Cho announced that he was going to start the home cell groups again, some of the men thought he was crazy. He called the few effective women leaders to his office, and they encouraged him, "We do not know how to preach a sermon. Teach us what we are to say, and then let us carry your message to our groups."

So every Wednesday before the evening service, Dr. Cho began to meet with willing women group leaders. He taught and distributed lessons to them, including an outline of what they should share at the next weekly home meeting. He also gave them a general outline for how the home meetings should run. They were to start with an opening prayer and the Apostles' Creed, followed by a time of singing. After concert prayer, the leader would preach or teach from the Word of God. An offering would be taken, then prayer for needs and concerns. After closing prayer, refreshments were to be served.

For a short time, all seemed well. Then new problems emerged. The group meetings had been rotating to a different home every week. Each home served refreshments, but competition developed as hostesses tried to outdo each other by serving more or better food. Some meetings deteriorated into long "religious parties," keeping wives from doing housework and irritating their time-conscious husbands. Several groups' geographical areas were so large that some leaders complained about the lengthy bus rides necessary to visit and minister to group members.[3] Some leaders still invited outside speakers who taught conflicting doctrines. In some groups, members started borrowing money from each other, and even pooled money in what later proved to be bad investments. At least one leader pilfered money from the offering. A few groups grew as large as fifty people, more people than one leader could care for adequately. Older leaders grew weary with the problems and dropped out.

Dr. Cho responded by setting clear guidelines. Refreshments should be simple and inexpensive, served at the end of a one-hour meeting that consistently followed a set format. During the meetings two roles would be rotated: Besides the leader, one person would be appointed that meeting's presider, opening the meeting by reading a thought-provoking Scripture passage and making sure the meeting stayed on course. Another person would be appointed that meeting's prayer captain and lead at least one occasion of prayer. No outside speakers would be allowed without prior approval. Money would not be borrowed or invested with anyone else in the group. Both the leader and an appointed group treasurer would count the offering, and a designated treasurer was to take it to the church. Dr. Cho recruited younger and stronger layleaders. When a group reached fifteen, an assistant was appointed; and they divided the group in half. After each meeting, leaders completed a written report to the church.[4]

The home groups finally began to grow in number and stability. In 1967, more than a hundred groups were in operation. In 1974, Dr. Cho finally felt his full health return. By January 1994, YFGC reported thirty-two thousand cell groups and more than seventy thousand layleaders ministering to a congregation of over seven hundred thousand.

The Spiritual Dynamics of Home Cell Groups

After the home cell groups became the fabric of the church, YFGC changed. Church became more than an event to attend. It became a community to belong to.

Through the past thirty years YFGC has learned that the most important aspect of the home cell groups is their spiritual dynamic. Participants consider cell groups a means to worship God, learn His Word, and experience His miracle power. One main goal of the groups is to help people personally encounter the supernatural God. A cell group leader told me, "In most communities the groups are known as places where miracles occur and problems are solved."

I remember when several cell groups invited Dad to speak at a special combined meeting. It would not be a quick journey, for they were twenty-five miles from the church, requiring Dad to make a one-and-a-half-hour drive through slow and heavy traffic. When Dad and Area Staff Pastor Lee neared their destination, they realized they had misplaced the exact address. With open windows they slowly drove down one street. The singing of Christian hymns and spirited handclapping drew them to the right home. The owner of that home greeted them. He had come to this newly developed area three and a half years before and had started the first cell group there. Now there were thirty-six cell groups in that community, with six hundred participants.

Over sixty people had packed into the crowded living room, including fifteen men who had arranged to be away from important jobs. Many who attended this combined meeting were cell leaders, including the twenty-seven women cell leaders and nine men cell leaders from the area.

After a time of prayer and song, the meeting was turned over to Dad. He preached from John 11 about the death of Lazarus and the resurrection power of Jesus, as Staff Pastor Lee interpreted. Later, Dad said, "My task was an easy one—to motivate people already motivated, and inspire people already growing in faith."

After the message, Dad and Pastor Lee prayed and laid hands on those who had gathered. Several received the baptism in the Holy Spirit. One woman with a tumor in her stomach reported that she felt a burning sensation when she received prayer and that she could no longer feel the tumor.

When the people stopped praying, a Mr. Kang gave his testimony. He had been a gangster, living on thievery and extortion. The scar still remained where he had slashed his stomach with a beer bottle before an audience of frightened policemen. At that time his mother visited YFGC, accepted Christ, and turned from her traditional Korean idolatry. After the weeks and months of her insistence, Mr. Kang finally agreed to go with her to an all-night prayer meeting and later to Prayer Mountain. While there, he entered a saving relationship with Jesus Christ and was set free from the binding habits of his old way of life. "I am so happy now," Mr. Kang said. "I thank God for my freedom in Jesus Christ and for the men in my weekly cell group."

Rotating Host Homes

YFGC finds it important to rotate the location of cell meetings, with groups meeting each week in a different home. There are two reasons for this rotation. First, New Testament Christians met "from house to house" (Acts 2:46, KJV), implying the rotation of homes in the Early Church. The second reason is expressed in the words of one woman I met: "We believe that when Christians worship God in a home, that home is blessed."

Because of this belief, group members often target their host or hostess in that meeting's prayers. Sometimes, when a person is sick or in difficulty—even a willing unbeliever—the group meets in that person's home, and during the meeting pray for his healing or problem. The unwritten rule is that no home should host a group more than once a month.

A new YFGC member told me, "I was a nominal Buddhist, who for the past several months had been struggling with chronic bronchitis. When people from the neighborhood women's cell group invited me to church, I refused. But when they told me that Jesus heals today, they had my attention. So when they asked if the cell group could meet the next week in my home and pray for my healing, I agreed. During that cell group meeting, even though the singing and praying were different from what I was used to, I felt more peace than I ever thought possible. When they prayed for me, I wasn't instantly healed, but felt much better. The real healing occurred when I received Jesus Christ as my personal Lord and Savior. I haven't had another bout with bronchitis now for nearly a year."

Homogenous Home Cell Groups

Through the years, YFGC developed four types of homogenous groups—men, women, youth, and children; most of the people were also similar in occupation or close in age. This has aided the evangelistic effort of the groups, for they easily know whom to target: people like those in their group.[5]

The men's groups began in 1968 by Chulik Lee. Spurred by the growing success of the women's groups and concerned for the men of the church, Lee began the first men's home group in the spacious living room of a man named Changshick Ahn. Only five men attended the first men's home group meeting, but twenty to thirty men attended later meetings. They soon split into two groups, and Lee announced their success. Soon men throughout the church started home groups.

Although some of the men's groups meet in offices and businesses, most meet in homes. Most men in these groups either work for companies or have their own businesses. Some men's groups meet in offices and factories, using this as an opportunity to reach non-Christian coworkers. However, most men's groups meet in the evening after a day of work. The favorite time for the men's groups is on Saturday night. Many also like to meet at eight on Friday nights, later to join in the Friday all-night prayer meeting at the church. Their wives are welcome to join the meeting as well.

One significant addition to the groups came in 1978. At Dad's prompting, YFGC developed the children's home cell groups. Children's groups often meet after school on Fridays, or after half a day of school on Saturdays, in the home of their adult children's leader. An estimated 70 percent of the more than twenty-five thousand children involved in these groups come from homes where the parents are not believers. These groups form one of the most evangelistic outreaches of the church. The children themselves do most of the outreach, bringing friends to the teacher's neighborhood home to hear about Jesus.

Youth (young adult) groups began in 1980 for single-adult factory workers who could not participate in the regular men's and women's cells. Youth groups customarily meet during the factory lunch hour or in a single's apartment after a day of work. Ten years after they began, nearly a thousand cell groups ministered to young adults ranging in age from twenty-one to thirty-five. The diligent members of one youth cell so impressed the management of a confectionery factory that it asked the church to send more people "just like those youth cell members" for workers.

But the most prevalent groups—in 1993 numbering twenty-eight thousand—remain the women's groups. Since 70 percent of married women in South Korea are full-time homemakers, most still meet in women's groups.[6] The women's groups usually meet at homes during the day, when husbands are at work and children are in school. Toddlers and infants are either brought to the meeting or left with relatives living in the same household. The women reach out to other women, leading to the phrase repeated often in YFGC: "The secret to winning a family to Jesus is to start with the wife." Even now, women of the church have a reputation for "praying their husbands through" to a saving relationship with Jesus Christ.

Starting New Home Cell Groups

Yunhi Kim has participated in cell groups since 1967, when

she was sixteen. "When the church moved to Yoido in 1973," Yunhi explained, "we had a large building to fill. Cell meetings spent less time in fellowship and more in evangelism. Most of our leaders now are active young homemakers who search for people with problems. Most groups have developed a reputation in their communities. People with problems or sicknesses know that they can come to a group and receive prayer. Even non-Christians come expecting God to do miracles in their lives."

One person who has often been involved in starting new home groups is Duchun Cho, father of Dr. Yonggi Cho. He has been active in the church since 1971, serving most of his retirement years as an elder and regularly practicing visitation that often results in the start of new home cell groups.

On a cool winter day, the eighty-year-old Duchun Cho reminisced with me, "Six days every week, from morning until evening, I have spent more than twenty years making home ministry visits. I have gone to pray for and comfort the sick, the poor, and those with problems. Sometimes people would ask me to come. Other times I would go on my own and search out people who wanted me to pray with them. It was in home visitation that I learned how we are to be with one another, 'to rejoice with those who rejoice, and to mourn with those who mourn' [Romans 12:15]. I have lived long enough to see much fruit from making home ministry visits."

When there was not a cell group in an area, he went alone in visitation, primarily to the homes of sick or problem-ridden unbelievers. When the person was sick or the problem difficult, he often visited and prayed for that person every day. Many were healed and later born again. At that point he then helped with the formation of a cell group in that area. He was able to help start many cell groups in that way.

Not all cell groups and cell leaders are equally evangelistic, however. Districts vary in some processes and approaches. One district pastor told me they had two basic approaches in starting a cell group. One approach is aggressively evangelistic. They assign a leader to a neighborhood, and he visits every home in that area. As he leads others to Jesus, the group is born and grows. He said, "These are the cells and leaders which bring rapid growth to YFGC. In our district about one-third of the leaders have used this approach."

He continued, "The other two-thirds of the leaders are good, stable Christian models but are not as aggressive. When we have two believers in an area, we place one of these leaders with them. When that group gradually grows to nine or ten, we designate someone in that group as an assistant and then divide the group. As much as possible, we divide groups based on natural networks. For example, if the assistant in that group brought two other cell members to the Lord, then that individual will split off with those members to start a new group. If there are no natural networks, then we divide the groups based on geography."

Components of Home Cell Groups

PRAYER

Why would people who live thirty miles from YFGC band together, form groups, and reach out to others? A concept consistently voiced in the home groups is this: "Find a need and meet it. Find a problem and solve it. Find a sick person and pray in faith for his healing." The group commits to pray for a person until God's miracle power is released on his behalf.

For groups to experience God's miracle power, prayer must permeate each meeting, including prayer for the concerns or needs of any non-Christians present. Chulik Lee, the leader of a men's cell group, said there have been some instant healings in his group but that most of the healings have been gradual. One man in the group had a stroke and was paralyzed on his left side. The group continued to pray for him until he was completely healed and walked freely again.

GOD'S WORD

Through the years, focus on the Word of God has remained central to both church worship services and the cell meetings. Believers often repeat Romans 10:17—"Faith comes from hearing the message, and the message is heard through the Word of Christ."

In 1980, YFGC's Institute for Full Gospel Education (called Youngsan Institute and now the Education Division [see chapter 8]) developed the first of a series of seven study guides for the home cell groups. This series provides a systematic study of the Bible over a seven-year period.[7] The content of these study guides was based on more than four hundred of Dr. Cho's sermons, primarily his Wednesday evening expository preaching. They were edited by a staff of theologically trained pastors. By 1987 the groups had completed their first cycle, returning the next year to the first volume of the series. Each lesson focuses on one basic and relevant biblical truth.

Format for Weekly Study Guide Lesson

Objectives: Each lesson has two to four main objectives. The leader keeps these clear in his mind throughout the Bible study.

Today's Scripture: This is the main text for the lesson; the group reads this portion of Scripture aloud together.

Memory Verse: Central to the lesson this verse is read aloud together by the group three or four times.

Leading Questions: Usually the leader asks two to three observation questions of the group about the Scripture verses read.

Today's Message: Two to three pages in length, this narrative explains the week's topic. In most groups, people take turns reading paragraphs of this narrative section aloud until the entire message has been read. After each person reads, the leader will often make comments on significant points, sometimes interjecting personal examples.

Closing Questions: The leader asks three closing questions that will draw the material from the lesson together.

Application: The lesson ends with two to three suggestions for applying the message to daily life.

One woman who discovered the importance of applying God's Word is Kyongboon Shin. Kyongboon hated her father and had frequently told him so, for he had mistreated her mother and had gambled away family finances.

At one weekly cell meeting, the lesson was on the importance of forgiveness and the danger of holding bitterness. For the first time, Kyongboon clearly understood that because Jesus Christ had forgiven her, she was to forgive others. During the time of group prayer, Kyongboon asked Jesus to help her, and she chose to forgive her father.

The following week, Kyongboon contacted her father and told him about her change of heart. He was delighted. Kyongboon invited him to church, and he readily accepted. That next Sunday, Kyongboon's father accepted Jesus Christ as his Lord and Savior.

"I didn't realize it then," Kyongboon said, "but my bitterness affected how I acted and had blocked my father from coming to Jesus. My forgiveness paved the way for his salvation. My family has never been happier. I am so grateful for the Bible truths I learn in my cell meetings."

FELLOWSHIP

At the end of each meeting, after the hour format is complete, the host or hostess serves simple refreshments, giving opportunity for believers to share their personal testimonies with any visitors.

Once I attended a men's cell group led by Mr. Jungoon Chea, a businessman who served as a deacon in the church. During the time of refreshments, Mr. Chea introduced me to another visitor in the group, an English high-school teacher who said he was an agnostic. As we sat around a table of cookies and soft drinks, we shared our testimonies, telling what Jesus Christ had done in our lives. The English teacher did not make a decision for Jesus Christ that night, but the smile on his face and his quick agreement to return to the next meeting was proof to us that the Holy Spirit was dealing with him.

Home Ministry Visits

From its start, YFGC has placed high value both on what happens during group meetings and on what group leaders do between the meetings. For this reason, staff pastors encourage leaders to minister to others through home ministry visits to group participants and to target unbelievers with the gospel message.

Elder Cho stated, "Home visits to members can help them grow spiritually. When there already was a cell group in an area, I would take the cell leader with me when I did visitation. Home cell groups and home visitation are closely related. If the two are not operating together, both the Christians and the group will be weak."

The Bible says much about ministering to others. Throughout

the New Testament are dozens of "one another" Scripture passages.[8] YFGC teaches that we are not to limit this "one another" dynamic to other believers. The point of Jesus' Parable of the Good Samaritan is that love is to have no boundaries. Jesus further told us to "go and make disciples of all nations," to "go into all the world and preach the good news to all creation" (Matthew 28:19; Mark 16:15). Believers at YFGC take the "one another" dynamic seriously, especially in the realms of prayer and evangelism.

Home Cell Meeting Format	
Praise	Silent prayer
	Apostles' Creed (in unison)
	Hymns or choruses (in unison; 7 minutes)
	Opening prayer
Communion with God	Bible study (30 minutes)
	Concert prayer (3 to 5 minutes)
Gratitude	Offering
	Prayer of thanks (5 minutes)
Fellowship	Concert prayer
	Introduction of new converts and guests
	Hymn
Closing	The Lord's Prayer (sung in unison; 2 minutes)
This generally is the format, but the program may be shifted from time to time.	

THE IMPACT OF PRAYER AND SCRIPTURE READING

Most group leaders not only coordinate a weekly meeting but also make weekly home ministry visits.[9]

What happens in these visits? Staff pastors and layleaders agree that the reading of Scripture and prayer are top priorities. One added, "The most important thing to do before going on a visit is to pray. Sometimes God will impress you with the real problem you will face, even before you go. Other times, He will give you specific guidance during the visit about what Scripture to read and what to say. We have found it best to pray for at least one hour before making visits."

Mrs. Han, a cell leader, visited the home of Poknam Pak. Poknam was confined to her bed after having suffered a stroke. Mrs. Han read aloud from the Bible to Poknam, "He was pierced for our transgressions, he was crushed for our iniquities; the punishment that brought us peace was upon him, and by his wounds we are healed" (Isaiah 53:5). Then she prayed for the woman to be healed. Poknam felt an immediate improvement. After that, other members of her neighborhood cell group continued visiting and praying for Poknam's healing, and within three months she was walking.

Another woman who received a visit said, "I was deep in despair. It just seemed that nothing was going right. Then my cell leader visited me. God had given her a verse for me." The cell leader read, "Fear not, for I have redeemed you; I have summoned you by name; you are mine. When you pass through the waters, I will be with you; and when you pass through the rivers, they will not sweep over you. When you walk through the fire, you will not be burned; the flames will not set you ablaze" (Isaiah 43:1–2).

The woman said, "I cannot tell you how much that Scripture meant to me. We prayed after that, and I was much encouraged. Things soon began to change. God's Word is powerful."

JOINING HANDS WITH THE SAVIOR

"For twenty years," said Elder Duchun Cho, "home visitation has been my delight. Some like to see movies, others like to climb mountains, but my primary joy and delight has been in visiting homes—to pray for the sick to be healed, to comfort the despondent, to encourage those with problems, to befriend the lonely. It is through prayer in home visitation that we join the hand of the weak and problem-ridden to the hand of our powerful Savior."

One woman asked Elder Cho to visit the home of her older sister, Sookyong, who had graduated from medical school in the Sorbonne in France. Sookyong, a medical professor, discovered she had stomach cancer in the final stage. She was skeptical when Elder Cho came and prayed for her, but she said, "I felt something happen in my stomach while you were praying. This is strange!"

For the first time in months, Sookyong could sit up in bed. She said, "I didn't believe in prayer or divine healing, but now I feel a difference."

Sookyong began going to church, first carried on a pallet and later walking on her own. Her healing continued, and she decided to receive Jesus Christ as her Lord and Savior. When she went for an examination, an amazed doctor told her the cancer was completely gone.

Elder Cho also visited a paralyzed man living with his son's family. The family had grown weary taking care of the stroke victim, but Elder Cho came to visit the man every day. As Elder Cho prayed for the man, he improved to the point he could sit up in bed. However, the greatest impact of those visits was on the man's family. Both the son and daughter-in-law were so impressed with the consistency of Elder Cho's care that they started going to church and became Christians. The son, Hyungyu Lee, later went to Bible school and now serves as pastor of a Korean church in the United States.

Chiyoun Kim became a Christian because Elder Cho visited her home. Later her husband, Jayoung Kang, became a Christian. He felt a call to the ministry, went on to Bible college, and now serves as pastor of a church in Pusan.

Another woman impacted by the church's visitation ministry was Myungsook Ahn. She was desperate. Her husband had lost his job and physically abused her when he drank. Their finances were almost gone. Even though she considered herself a religious person, no amount of idol worship relieved her personal pain.

Then the neighborhood cell and section leaders visited her. They had come to her house several times before, often bringing her a copy of the weekly church newspaper, *Full Gospel News.* She had talked briefly with them and once or twice had read a testimony of healing, but she had not really been interested.

That day was different. Myungsook's desperation was so keen that, through flowing tears, she told them her struggle. They explained, "God is the source of true happiness. If you confess your sins and receive Jesus Christ as your Savior, He will give you peace in your heart and in your family."

So that day Myungsook received Jesus Christ as her personal

Lord and Savior. In the weeks that followed, she went with her cell leader to church services and neighborhood cell meetings.

But her difficulties continued. Her brother was sent to jail for twenty days, her husband's second business failed, and they were forced to sell their home to pay some debts.

Members of her cell group banded together and provided Myungsook and her husband with a three-room rental unit. Her cell leader helped her find temporary work. They remained in earnest prayer for Myungsook's situation.

Soon Myungsook's husband started a new job, and their finances improved. He later became a Christian and faithfully attended church. Myungsook's rebellious brother was also born again. Myungsook now joyfully leads a women's cell group in her community and is quick to reach others with the gospel message.

"I thank Jesus Christ," Myungsook often says, "who forgave my sins and restored my family. I also am deeply grateful to my cell group leader and the members of my cell group. It would be impossible to say how important they have been to my life."

A Plan of Evangelism

People involved in cell meetings openly say that the most outstanding feature of YFGC's cell groups is their ardent evangelism, focusing on unsaved friends, acquaintances, and neighbors. While a small number of the groups (an estimated 10 percent) meet in offices and businesses, the great majority meet in homes, concentrating much of their energy on evangelism in the surrounding neighborhood and community.

One staff pastor told me, "For the cell leader, evangelism is to be like breathing. You are to evangelize whenever and wherever you can."

YFGC encourages each cell group to win at least one person to the Lord every six months. Once a year, at the close of the fall semiannual cell and section leaders' conference, Dr. Cho recognizes and prays for the leaders who have won the most people to the Lord that previous year.[10]

The church places great importance on follow-up of new converts, on those for whom the people have prayed. When Jesus spoke the word, Lazarus rose from the dead. Yet, the story did not end there, for Lazarus was still wrapped in his grave clothes.

Jesus told those around Lazarus, "Take off the grave clothes and let him go" (John 11:44). YFGC teaches that many are still wrapped in "grave clothes"—old ways of ungodly thinking and behavior. They need someone to help untie them. Perhaps this is why the writer of Galatians stated, "Bear one another's burdens, and so fulfill the law of Christ" (Galatians 6:2).

One man who needed someone to bear his burdens in prayer was Jaekun Yu. Jaekun had a shop near the storefront owned by Deacon Pak. Pak began sharing with Jaekun about Jesus Christ. His genuine witness challenged Jaekun to evaluate his life. Jaekun finally went to church with Deacon Pak, and in that first service made a decision to receive Jesus Christ as his Savior.

However, even though Jaekun started to attend church every Sunday, he continued to go drinking with his buddies. Early one Christmas morning, as he stumbled drunkenly across a road, a car struck him. The collision threw him fifteen feet into the air, breaking nine ribs and fracturing his pelvis. A ruptured liver and internal bleeding resulted in low blood pressure. His abdomen swelled like a balloon. Yet somehow he clung to life. When he regained consciousness, Jaekun thought of his wife and little children and how he might not see them again. He prayed, "God forgive me. Give me another chance."

He underwent six hours of surgery. Then for five days and nights, he slipped in and out of consciousness. Finally, a doctor came in and gently broke the news to Jaekun. He would live but would never walk again.

Deacon Pak and a section leader came to visit Jaekun often, praying with him and leaving him tapes of Dr. Cho's sermons. Deacon Pak told him, "As you pray, picture yourself healthy, walking without any difficulty!"

One day Deacon Pak strode into Jaekun's hospital room. He stood by his bed and squared his shoulders. "I have been praying for you, Jaekun. I think you are ready. Now . . . get up and walk!"

It seemed impossible, but Jaekun lifted his limp legs over the side of the bed. He stood up, swaying a little, then took a step. Then another, and another. Soon, he was marching around the room, laughing and praising God.

By the time he was released in February, Jaekun was completely healed. "I repented of all my sins in that hospital room," Jaekun recalls. "I was so thankful to God that I gave the entire settlement money from the accident in the offering. Now I use Christmas as the date to celebrate my 'birthday,' the day of my true repentance and making Jesus Lord as well as Savior of my life. I am grateful to God for my healing and grateful that Deacon Pak and others were praying for me."

Setting Goals

My interviews with district pastors, subdistrict pastors, section leaders, and cell leaders revealed several steps in many cells' evangelism process.

First, the cell group is to identify a target area, or a list of target people, and set goals. YFGC considers God-prompted visions, dreams, and goals to be part of the language and initial workings of the Holy Spirit. Each cell leader is to pray that God will give him a specific number he and his group are to win to Jesus Christ that year. Each year staff pastors also set evangelistic goals for their districts, encouraging the layleaders they work with to do the same. Usually a cell leader targets a limited geographical area, typically the neighborhood he and cell members live in. At other times, cell and section leaders help members identify specific people to reach.

Early one year, during a weekly meeting with her eight cell leaders, Section Leader Okja Kim challenged them to win at least one person from a hundred families to the Lord. Her cell leaders grew silent and looked at her in disbelief. No one spoke a word.

Okja did not have any paper with her. So she took a drugstore calendar off the wall, ripped off eight pages, and gave one to each cell leader. "On the blank back of these pages," she instructed, "write down your name and the names of all the target families you can think of. If we do this by faith, God will help us accomplish this goal."

Within ten minutes, those eight cell leaders collectively wrote more than seventy names. "That was the start of the process," recalled Okja. "By the end of the year we had led people from 122 different families to Jesus."

PRAYING PERSISTENTLY

Okja says that they quickly found that evangelism without prayer was not effective. So she and her cell leaders spent the next month praying each day for the names of those they had targeted.[11]

Cell leaders point to the Scripture verse that teaches how Satan has "blinded the minds of unbelievers, so that they cannot see the light of the gospel" (2 Corinthians 4:4). They teach that when prayer has resulted in the bombardment of the enemy's spiritual blinding, the unbeliever will be more receptive to the gospel and the believer will be more effective and bold in sharing the light of Jesus.

One cell leader told me of meeting a Buddhist who was so sick he could not eat. The cell leader let him know that she was going to pray for his healing. She prayed diligently for him every day for one week. At the end of the week, the man was healed. He later gave his life to Jesus and now serves as a cell leader in his area.

GIVING GOSPEL LITERATURE

Prayer without action profits little. Most section and cell leaders visit neighborhood homes at least one day each week. Some of these visits are to the homes of group members. They usually spend two to three hours in evangelistic visitation, with the section and cell leaders going to every home in that neighborhood.

Some section and cell leaders report that they make visits two days each week. One day a week they visit the homes of believers who need ministry. The other day they focus on evangelistic visitation. Some evangelistic layleaders visit up to five days every week.

However, not all leaders find that a weekly visitation is well received. Some have discovered they must use other approaches to establish caring relationships.

One cell leader grew weary when she visited the apartments in her building and doors were repeatedly slammed in her face. As she later prayed and poured out her frustration to God, she sensed the Holy Spirit gently say, "Just show them love."

So she went to the one place that most people in that high-rise apartment building had to go—the elevator. She rode up and down the elevator two to three hours every day. When people entered, she greeted them with a smile and a kind word. If a woman had groceries or restless children, she helped carry anything she could. This cell leader showed love in every way possible.

People eventually began responding. As she established caring relationships with her neighbors, many of them invited her to their apartments for refreshments and conversation, and she later invited them to her next cell meeting. Within two months, one person came to the Lord. Within a year, she and other Christian homemakers led more than a hundred people to Jesus in that apartment complex.

However, most leaders have found brief, weekly visits to unbelievers to be highly effective. "As I continued to be consistent in stopping by unbelievers' homes each week and giving them copies of the church newspaper," Okja Kim told me, "relationships developed with certain members of the families we had targeted. After we came to know each other a little bit, they began conversing with me.

"At that point," Okja explained, "I talked with them only at their doors. After doing this for one or two months, I ended each brief visit by asking, 'Before I go, would it be all right if I stood in your doorway and said a short prayer of blessing over your home?'

"No one denied that prayer. When I returned home, I prayed and stormed heaven, asking God to allow those people to see some unexpected good thing happen in their family and home. The next time I stopped by, I told them I had been praying for them. Many times they invited me in for a cup of tea or coffee."

When leaders visit unbelievers, they usually take at least one piece of Christian literature to give them. The tool used most often is the four-page *Full Gospel News*, which contains a summary of Dr. Cho's previous Sunday sermon, notes for the upcoming home cell meeting, at least one personal testimony of healing or salvation, and assorted church news.[12] One section leader explained that she also gives copies of either a monthly Christian magazine or one of Dr. Cho's sermon books to unbelievers as her expression of interest. One subdistrict pastor instructs leaders to write their names and phone numbers on each piece of literature given, so they can be contacted if that person has a need.

One example of people affected by Christian literature is that of Professor Siwoo Lee and his wife. When they were young, they had occasionally attended church. After their marriage, they became caught up in the social and academic life of professors of Seoul National University, the "Harvard" of Korea. God, church, and spiritual matters were of no concern to them.

Then Yunghu Yu, a women's cell leader in their neighborhood, met Mrs. Lee. Each week for the next five years, Yu made a brief visit to Mrs. Lee, giving her a copy of the *Full Gospel News*. Mrs. Lee would later give the copy to her husband. Unknown to her, Professor Lee carefully read and kept each copy. After five years, the Lees decided to commit their lives to Jesus Christ.

Once when I visited the Lees, Professor Lee, then eighty-one years old, proudly took me to a room with three cardboard boxes full of copies of the *Full Gospel News,* which he had read and saved through those years. Professor Lee and his wife continue to grow in their Christian walk, and are now anxious for their adult children to come to a saving relationship with their risen Lord.

FINDING PEOPLE WITH NEEDS

Okja found something else that helped in bringing people to the Savior: "When I talked with these people we had targeted to evangelize," she said, "I discovered one thing. If a person ever told me of a need or problem, it let me know that person was receptive. It never failed that I could then lead that person to faith in Jesus Christ."

The ultimate aim of evangelistic visitation is to find people with needs and problems and then lead them to the Problem Solver, Jesus Christ. A subdistrict leader, Leebu Pak, tells her cell leaders, "Look for problems. When you find someone with a problem, you are almost guaranteed that person will come to Jesus."

A frequent practice of female cell and section leaders is called "holy eavesdropping." The leader keeps her ears open, especially in places where her neighbors shop or congregate. If she overhears a conversation mentioning a need or difficulty, she makes a mental note and begins to pray for that person and that concern. After prayer, she might then visit that woman with fruit or flowers, plus that week's copy of the church newspaper. In response to the gift, the woman often invites the leader inside for tea or coffee. In the process of conversation, trust is developed and the warm, caring attitude of the leader puts the woman at ease. When the woman expresses a need or difficulty, the cell leader shares her testimony of how Jesus met her own needs and how He is concerned with people's daily problems.

Encouraging Church Involvement

After a leader has established a caring relationship with an unbeliever, he or she may invite the person to a cell meeting or church service.

The relationship of YFGC's worship services to the cell group meetings can be compared to romance and the marriage ceremony. A challenge to every home cell group is to "romance" those in their community for Jesus; however, the public declaration of one's faith, like the public wedding ceremony, best takes place in the church building. Dr. Cho ends his sermons by asking all who want to become Christians to stand. Those who stand usually have one or more Christian friends, often from their cell group, sitting next to them. Church services and cell group meetings partner together to knit seekers and new believers into the larger body of Christ.

Section Leader Kim recounted, "Even after I've discovered an area of need and become trusted by an unbeliever, I find that she may still make excuses when I invite her to church. So instead, I bring her to several cell group meetings. In the cell meetings, members pray for any problems she has. Cell members expect answers to prayer and show her love."

She continued, "At that point, the unbeliever usually asks why I don't take her to church sometime. I gladly agree to do so. Many receive Jesus during the call to salvation near the end of a church service. After the service, I take her to my district office and introduce her to my subdistrict pastor. The subdistrict pastor then prays with the newcomer. When she leaves the church, she does not feel lost in a large crowd but recognized and cared for."

Most Koreans do not own private cars but use public buses for transportation. Some areas are distant from YFGC, requiring multiple bus changes with up to two hours' travel time. If a subdistrict is distant from the church, the local members rent buses to four of the Sunday services. Those who ride pay their portion, often also paying for the non-Christian friends they accompany to the service.

The most ardent cell and section leaders come to three services on Sunday, each time bringing a different unbeliever. Some bring more than one unbeliever to a single service. Once, Shin brought so many women with her that one older woman was afraid of getting separated and lost in the crowd. So they tied a long cord around the right wrist of each woman; that day no one was lost.

There are some who will come to a group meeting who will not yet consider going to a church service. Yongshik Lee had been raised a Buddhist but had grown skeptical of any religion. Several people had invited him to church, but he always refused. Yongshik didn't care how good a pastor's sermons were supposed to be or how small or large a church was; he had decided he would never darken the door of any church or temple.

Then some men in his neighborhood befriended him. Two were businessmen with families like himself, so he readily identified with them. When they asked Yongshik to join them in their weekly men's home cell group meeting, Yongshik thought, *Why not? It can't hurt. Besides, this man's house is right down my street.*

So Yongshik went that week. The singing was lively, the prayer spirited, and the lesson interesting. Even though it was different from going drinking with his buddies from the office, Yongshik sensed that these men had a joy in life that he badly wanted. So when they invited him to return next week, Yongshik agreed. "I'm still not going to any church," he told them, "but this home meeting . . . well, it's different."

So for the next two years, Yongshik went to nearly every weekly men's cell group meeting in his neighborhood. Finally, in the midst of his Christian friends, whom he had come to trust, Yongshik's defenses melted. During a cool autumn night's meeting, Yongshik received Jesus Christ as his Lord and Savior.

The next Sunday Yongshik went with his elated friends to a worship service at YFGC. After the sermon, when Dr. Cho asked those who wanted to become Christians to stand and repeat a sinner's prayer, Yongshik stood. "I'm going public with this," he whispered to the men's cell group leader next to him.

Over the following years, Yongshik was faithful in both church and cell meeting attendance, his family later following him in the faith. Yongshik Lee now serves in the church as both a deacon and a men's home cell group leader.

DISCIPLING NEW BELIEVERS

Once a person attends the cell meetings and church services and makes a commitment to Jesus Christ, the church's process is still not complete. Both that area's district staff pastor and section layleader visit the new convert at home. During that visit, the subdistrict pastor shares his and others' testimonies of how they became born again. He often has the new convert once more repeat a sinner's prayer and spends time encouraging the new believer in the Christian walk.

I remember going on one new convert visit and being impressed by how the staff pastor carefully explained the importance of daily Bible reading, even to the point of asking the man to bring out his new Bible so he might be shown how to find Scripture references, as well as one approach to Bible study. If the new convert has any problems, the staff pastor ends the time with prayer.

That area's section leader goes with the subdistrict pastor on such visits. If the new convert is not already involved in a cell group, the section leader assesses the person's age, educational background, and preferences. On that basis the section leader decides which of the five to ten groups in the area the new believer would most likely enjoy and receive the most relevant ministry from.

The next week the section leader and the leader of the chosen cell group visit that new convert, and the section leader introduces him to the cell leader. Often the next cell meeting is held in the new believer's home, and he will be welcomed into the group.

Dr. Cho has this perspective about the purpose of cell groups at YFGC: "Our cell group system is a net for our Christians to cast. Instead of a pastor fishing for one fish at a time, organized believers form nets to gather hundreds and thousands of fish. A pastor should never try to fish with a single rod but should organize believers into the 'nets' of a cell system." (See also Appendix 3: Three Kinds of Group Systems.)

6

The Ministry of the Pastoral Staff

In the early days, when the church was under a tent, there were three staff pastors: Dr. Cho, Jashil Choi, and, later, my father, John Hurston. Yet, even though they started with a small staff, they set patterns that have continued throughout YFGC's history. One pattern was daily home ministry visits. They visited throughout the community, putting special emphasis on contacting the sick, the poor, and the struggling.

"I remember one woman we led to the Lord during a home ministry visit in those days," said Dr. Cho, reminiscing. "Her husband was an agnostic high school teacher and did not like us visiting his wife and praying with her. The woman had been in a religious cult. So we not only led her to the Lord, but we also prayed for her to be delivered from Satan's bondage."

This couple had more money than most, enough to even afford a housekeeper. One day, while working on the roof, this housekeeper slipped and fell to the ground, where she lay lifeless. The husband was so desperate that he mimicked the way he had seen Dr. Cho and the team pray in home visitation. He leaned over the housekeeper's still body and rebuked the devil in the name of Jesus. The housekeeper suddenly regained consciousness. The high school teacher became a Christian and started attending the church.

My parents also went on home visits. They visited many people, some in cement block homes but most in houses made of pasteboard. Wherever they went, their message was the same: Jesus came to save, to bless, and to meet needs.

Early Home Ministry Visits

In the home visits, they sang a hymn, read from the Bible, and told testimonies of others who had been touched by God. When a person was sick, they went again and again, praying for his or her healing. The new church grew quickly because people who were healed told their neighbors, inviting them to come and hear the team when they returned to their house. By the next visit, the team was able to share God's love and power to a crowded room. Word of healings spread, and more people started coming to the tent church, bringing sick friends and neighbors with them.

Once, Jashil Choi heard about a woman whose farmer husband had just died. Jashil went into the woman's field and helped her harvest their ripened rice, singing hymns as she worked. Jashil's practical concern impressed the widow, and she later became a Christian.

In 1961, when the church made the transition to Sodaemoon, they began dealing with larger numbers of people. Still, focus on staff pastors making ministry visits did not lessen. Before the church's dedication in February 1962, Jashil Choi and eighteen women visited a thousand homes, inviting people to attend the upcoming dedication crusade. By this time, a visitation elder had been added to the pastoral staff, making a total of four ministry staff members. They spent two days each week in the church office, where long lines of people waited for prayer and counseling.

Dr. Cho and Dad visited people in their homes every Thursday and Friday. Dad recalled one of those visits: "One cold autumn day, Dr. Cho and I walked near the top of a mountain to find the shanty of a poor family who had started attending our church. We sat on the dirt floor of their one-room home and ministered to them. Just then, we heard what sounded like the cries of a baby from nearby."

After they concluded that visit, they looked for the source of the crying. Dr. Cho and Dad hurried through the brisk wind and found a tiny, roofless pasteboard structure, where a mother huddled with her crying toddler. It was so cold. The cardboard walls did nothing to keep out the piercing wind. The woman's face was streaked with tears.

Dad and Dr. Cho quietly walked in and began talking with her. Her husband had been killed in the war, leaving her with three children. She was only thirty years old, but hard work and little food had already taken their toll. She looked like an old woman, sick and no longer able to work and support her family.

Dad continued, "Dr. Cho stooped and picked up that crying, dirty toddler and held her close against him until she got warm and stopped crying."

Finally, Dr. Cho and Dad returned to the church but sent others back to the widow on the mountain. Men built a roof, and women brought clothes and food for the widow and her children. The widow was so touched that she came to church and eventually gave her life to Jesus Christ. After she was physically healed, she returned to work as a street vendor, able to support her three children.

"The days we spent in the office praying and counseling with people were good," Dad later told me, "but they were not to compare with making home ministry visits. There is nothing like ministering to people where they live and work."

Setting Up a System of Home Visitation

Through the earlier days of the church, a staff pastor led most home ministry visits; however, as the church grew, the number of people requiring visits became too great. It was then that the pastoral staff, accompanied by layleaders, shifted their focus to visiting church members. It became the laypeople who took up the task of visiting unbelievers.

When the cell groups began in 1964, cell leaders became diligent in visitation, greatly multiplying the contacts with the unsaved. In 1970, when the congregation reached eight thousand, the church added three more pastors, both to oversee the growing number of cell groups and to help make home ministry visits. As numbers grew and many believers started their own businesses, another shift occurred. Not all ministry visits were made to homes, but also to places of business.

The church added a practice best translated "grand home visitation." In this thrust, the pastoral staff and layleaders systematically visited every member's home within a particular period of time.

Initially, each Grand Home Visitation lasted ten days and was done twice a year—in the spring and again in the fall. By the end of 1973, when the church had moved to Yoido Island, a pastoral staff of twenty ministered to a congregation of over twelve thousand. The following year the church divided Seoul into eight districts, each with its own pastoral staff. With the church's continued growth, Grand Home Visitation soon took a full month to complete. In 1981, the church estimated that 70,000 homes were visited by a pastoral staff of 220. By the mid-1980s, numbers had grown to the point that Grand Home Visitation took a full three months, and could be done only once a year—like a spiritual diagnostic checkup. By the late 1980s, the church added as many as seventy more pastors to the staff each year, simply to keep pace with the growing number of members.

Soon there was so much visitation to be done that staff pastors prioritized the types of visits to be made, putting visits to new believers at the top of their list. These visits were often done by layleaders as well. It became the policy that visits were to be made to new believers each week until they were established in the faith: baptized in water, baptized in the Holy Spirit, consistent in church and cell attendance, and faithful in tithing. The pastors also visited the sick, the poor, those with financial problems or other difficulties, the weak in faith, those who dropped out of church and cell groups, those who desired a prayer of blessing over business or family, and those who simply requested a home visit from a pastor. Zealous layleaders and church members carried out evangelistic visits to non-Christians.

As the church's growth spiraled, more pastors were added, but they never allowed visitation to slow down. In 1990, nearly all the over six hundred pastoral staff pastors were involved daily in visitation. That year, staff pastors made a recorded total of over six hundred thousand home ministry visits.

About 80 percent of the pastoral staff in the Department of Pastoral Care[1] work with the cell groups and spend the majority of their days making ministry visits. Most visits are scheduled so that the people know in advance when the pastor and layleader are coming and the time they have to leave.

Affecting Individual Lives

One wonders, in the midst of all these pastoral ministry visits, what personal effect these visits have had on the congregation. How has the activity of visitation affected individual lives?

Changsu Lee told me his story: "I was lonely. My wife had died eight years earlier, and all my children had left home except one—Hyongshik, who spent most of his time drunk. Since I was an atheist, it was unlikely that I would ever go to the senior citizen Bible classes at YFGC. But my Christian daughter-in-law, a cell group leader, signed me up. I was so lonely I agreed to go along."

Some of the pastors and layleaders noticed Changsu, so they visited him several times over the next few months. First, the staff pastor over his area came, accompanied by the male section leader of the community. Later the staff pastor over that area's district came. In each visit they had a short time of worship, shared relevant Bible passages, and prayed with Changsu. And almost every time they visited, Changsu's drunken son Hyongshik stumbled in to join them.

By the time Changsu completed the senior citizen's Bible classes, both he and Hyongshik had accepted Jesus Christ as their Lord and Savior. Hyongshik became sober, entered seminary, and is now in full-time ministry. Neither the old atheist nor the young drunk would have been considered likely prospects for most church visitation efforts. Nevertheless, Changsu's and Hyongshik's lives changed radically because determined pastoral staff pastors and layleaders went again and again to visit them.

Sometimes visitation teams have results of a different nature. Taesik Lee, a professor of English at Kukmin University, could no longer ignore his pain and physical weakness. When he finally saw a doctor, the diagnosis was the worst it could be—Professor Lee had cancer. But this news didn't deter the members of his fellowship group at the church. They came repeatedly to his home to sing praise songs, encourage Taesik with Scripture, and pray for his healing. Taesik is now healed, enjoying vibrant health.

Okrun Kim, a thirty-two-year-old relative of a church member, started exhibiting bizarre behavior—sitting around with a glassy-eyed stare, often flailing at the air. A team of five members from the church who had learned to do visitation by going with a staff pastor decided to visit Okrun. As they prayed with her, they sensed her problem was demonic.

They started to pray loudly, commanding the unclean spirit to come out. Suddenly, a harsh voice yelled out of Okrun, "Why are you casting me out?"

The visitation team increased the volume and the fervor of their praying. At that point Okrun stopped writhing, collapsed, and lost consciousness. A stench permeated the room, then faded. Okrun opened her eyes and gave them a bright smile. She readily received Jesus Christ as her Lord, Savior, and Deliverer. She has been normal ever since, with no similar incidents since her healing. She still talks about that visit to her home.

Former atheist Changsu, his minister son Hyongshik, healthy Professor Taesik, and vibrant Okrun have one thing in common—they were targets of YFGC's home visitation.

The Priority of Home Ministry Visits

Most churches and pastors in Korea practice home visitation. It is a way of life in that country's continuing revival. But few staff pastors in Korea practice ministry visits as frequently or as systematically as those at YFGC. And no church is larger.

YFGC considers ministry visitation a top priority for its pastoral staff and layleaders. They integrate ministry visitation into every part of church life. Nearly all the pastoral staff of more than seven hundred spend the bulk of their days in ministry visitation. An unpublished YFGC report reveals that the average staff pastor monthly spends sixteen days in visitation, making a total of ninety-one visits each month and more than a thousand ministry visits a year. Seeing the example of their staff pastors, the typical home group leader makes three to five home visits a week. Other layleaders make one home ministry visit weekly. In addition, each of the church's outreach fellowships has its own cadre of layleaders to make ministry visits. Doesn't so much visitation become overkill? What makes it meaningful is genuine concern for the welfare of each person visited. If the person to be visited is a church member, he or she is first called for an appointment. Visits to homes of unbelievers are made without calling first, since the purpose is to share the gospel and see them make a decision for Christ.

When I asked why home visitation is so important, staff pastors were surprised. One said bluntly, "It's in the Bible. Read it" (See the sidebars on pages 115 and 116). Praying, teaching, healing, having fellowship together—all these things were done in the homes of the Early Church. While corporate worship was also important to them, their focus on home ministry visits caused the new faith to spread rapidly, creating a vitality that rarely has been repeated. (See Appendix 4: Home Visitation in Church History.)

I asked a dozen YFGC staff pastors and layleaders, "What do you think would happen if home visitation were to stop suddenly at our church?" Each responded with a disbelieving gasp. Four finally said, "That's unthinkable! We always make ministry visits. We would never stop. Ministry visitation is like the eyes and ears of our church."

One female YFGC staff pastor pondered the question even longer and finally said, "If visitation stopped, I think our church would only be one-tenth its present size."

Dr. Cho asserts, "Ministry visitation is essential. When a person belongs to our congregation, he should be regularly visited by pastors and layleaders. Visitation is a key to a strong sense of unity and belonging within any church."

There is no doubt that the YFGC pastoral staff's ministry visitation is one of this church's primary keys to steady growth.

A Staff Pastor's Day

What would be the typical day of a staff pastor at the world's largest church? I determined to document a day in the life of a staff pastor, choosing to accompany and observe Kisuk Hong.

I had known Pastor Hong since he was appointed a deacon and cell leader in the church. I remembered him as diligent in his evening seminary classes. We had often talked, discussing everything from his wife and son to his desire to go into full-time ministry. Since he was now a YFGC staff pastor, I asked permission to go with him during a typical day. His English was limited, as was my Korean, but we always managed to communicate. At the time, Pastor Kisuk Hong served as a subdistrict pastor. He now serves as the head of the newly created Funeral Department overseeing and conducting funerals.

Jesus and Home Visitation

According to the Gospels, Jesus
- taught in homes (Mark 2:1–2; Luke 7:36; 10:38–41);
- gave instruction to His disciples in homes (Matthew 13:36; 17:25; Mark 7:17; 9:28–29,33–35; 10:10–12; John 13:2 to 17:26);
- went into a home to bring a dead girl back to life (Matthew 9:23–25; Mark 5:37–42; Luke 8:51–55);
- healed Peter's mother-in-law of a fever in a home (Matthew 8:14–15; Mark 1:29–31; Luke 4:38–39);
- healed the paralyzed man in a home (Mark 2:1–2);
- healed the man suffering from dropsy in a home (Luke 14:1–4);
- pronounced forgiveness of sins in two separate homes—once to a paralyzed man (Mark 2:1–5) and once to a sinful woman (Luke 7:36–37,48);
- spoke the Word to a woman who sought Him on behalf of her daughter and demons were cast out of her in a home (Mark 7:24–25,29–30);
- ate and enjoyed fellowship in a home, with at least five instances recorded in the New Testament (Matthew 9:10–13; 26:18–20; Mark 14:3; Luke 7:36; John 12:1–3);
- blessed the children in a home (Mark 9:33–37; 10:10,13–16);
- held the Last Supper in a room of a home (Matthew 26:18–19; Mark 14:14).

When Jesus sent out the twelve disciples and later the Seventy, He sent them in pairs into the homes of the villages and communities saying, "Whatever town or village you enter, search for some worthy person there and stay at his house until you leave" (Matthew 10:11; Luke 9:4; 10:1,5–7).

He told them to go into homes
- to preach the gospel (Matthew 10:7);
- to take authority over evil spirits (Matthew 10:1,8; Mark 6:7; Luke 9:1);
- to heal the sick (Matthew 10:1,8; Luke 9:1; 10:9);
- to raise the dead (Matthew 10:8);
- and to bless the home with peace (Matthew 10:13; Luke 10:5).

It is interesting that Jesus sent His disciples out in pairs (Mark 6:7; Luke 10:1). Perhaps this is reflective of Jesus' words in Matthew 18:19–20: "If two of you on earth agree about anything you ask for, it will be done for you by my Father in heaven. For where two or three come together in my name, there am I with them."

The disciples had dramatic results from their home visitation ministry. Many people heard the gospel, the sick were healed, and demons were cast out (Mark 6:12–13; Luke 9:6; 10:17).

At 8:30 in the morning, I meet Pastor Hong in his district office at the church. Thirteen gray desks line three sides of the spacious office; at each desk sits a staff pastor, busy writing or preparing for the coming day. Maps, charts, and written goals cover the walls.

I notice a chart above Pastor Hong's desk. This chart lists the eighteen section layleaders who help him oversee the 121 cell leaders in his ministry area. Another nearby chart documents 1,911 church members in his particular subdistrict.

Pastor Hong explains his regular schedule. Tuesday through Saturday, he arrives at the church by eight-thirty in the morning. Twice a week, the entire pastoral staff meet for devotions and prayer. The other days, they pray that first hour in their offices.

Home Visitation in the Early Church

Home visitation continued as a primary activity in the Early Church. Acts 5:42 reads, "Day after day, in the temple courts and from house to house, they never stopped teaching and proclaiming the good news that Jesus is the Christ."

The word "they" in Acts 5:42 is defined in verse 41: the apostles who had been persecuted by the Sanhedrin. This verse refutes the notion that the apostles spent all their time in prayer and Bible study. Instead, the apostles were relentless in home visitation, going from "house to house" to share God's Word.

Paul, outstanding among the apostles, declared in Acts 20:20, "You know that I have not hesitated to preach anything that would be helpful to you, but have taught you publicly and from house to house."

Emphasis on the home continued throughout the Early Church. Ananias visited Saul in a home to heal his blindness and ensure that he was filled with the Holy Spirit (Acts 9:11–18). Peter went into a home to bring dead Tabitha back to life (Acts 9:37–40). It was in a home that Paul healed Publius' sick father of dysentery. Many others who were sick then came to that home to have Paul pray for their healing (Acts 28:7–9).

Most staff pastors leave the church office by ten to begin a day of home and business ministry visits. The earliest Pastor Hong completes a day of visitation is at five-thirty in the evening, usually after making five to seven ministry visits. At least one day a week his visits extend into the evening to minister to working men in their homes.

Monday is family day, his only day off, when he rests from an active Sunday schedule with his wife and son. Once a month he accompanies other staff pastors, layleaders, and members from his district to their district's three-hour prayer and fasting service at Prayer Mountain.

As we talk, Pastor Hong completes his written report of visits he made the day before. He turns to give the report to his district pastor, who often goes on visitation with him.

Eighteen black notebooks line one side of Pastor Hong's desk—one for each of the sections under his oversight, with a separate page of information on each family and home cell group in that section.

This is the time for the annual Grand Home Visitation, when the pastors systematically make ministry visits to each church member in his or her home or business. Pastor Hong picks the notebooks for the two sections we will visit that day, places them in his briefcase, and we are off to our first visit.

I ask several questions as we ride in Pastor Hong's car, careful to record each point. He explains that he plans his schedule a month in advance. He spends one day a month with each of his lay "middle management" section leaders: on Tuesdays he meets with one section layleader, on Wednesdays with another, on Thursdays with a third, and so forth until he has gone on visitation with each of his eighteen section layleaders during that month. But on this day we will be with two section leaders.

Pastor Hong says that he meets each day's section leader at the first designated home by ten-thirty in the morning. Since the section layleader best knows the cell leaders of that area and is aware which church members are most in need of ministry, the section leader is responsible to arrange the appointments for the day; Pastor Hong's job is to minister. If the section leader has a full-time job, he or she arranges to be with the subdistrict pastor one day a month.

The first home we visit is modest. Section Leader Uhm, the middle management layleader who cares for the cell leaders and members in that area, greets Pastor Hong and directs him to the living room. He sits beside Senior Deaconess Kim, an older layleader who often accompanies him in visitation. This practice of taking a grandmotherly layleader keeps male staff pastors above reproach, especially when they visit women at home alone.

During the next two hours we visit four more homes. The lady in the first home is discouraged in her Christian walk. A five-year-old boy in the second home is in need of prayer. A young mother and her infant son are the focus of ministry in the third home. Those gathered in the fourth home are greatly encouraged by Pastor Hong's exhortation from Galatians 2:20.

Section Leader Uhm and Senior Deaconess Kim accompany Pastor Hong to each home and listen attentively to every word he speaks. When he counsels or preaches a short sermon, they mark their Bibles and take notes. The pattern of ministry in each home is much the same: Pastor Hong sits down with his accompanying layleaders, and all bow their heads in a moment of silent prayer. Pastor Hong then opens his black book on that section, turns to the page on that specific family, and asks a few questions to update the recorded information. Through this questioning process, he discovers an area of concern or struggle that needs ministry. Then he asks the senior deaconess to pray.

During her prayer, he quietly turns in his Bible to find the most appropriate passage. After the prayer ends, he asks the targeted person to read the selected passage. The next ten minutes he exhorts that person with the Word of God. Each visitation service concludes with a prayer of blessing for that person, family, and home.

As I watch in the fourth home, I write some of my own insights in a notebook: "When pastors preach on Sunday, they bring the light of God's Word to a congregation. But when a pastor shares the Word in a ministry visit, knowing the specific situation of that individual or family, it is more like concentrated laser light. One ministry visit seems worth a year of sermons."

When that visit ends, Pastor Hong says farewell to Section Leader Uhm. The senior deaconess and I get in the car with Pastor Hong for a ten-minute ride to the next section.

The fifth home this day is different. It is a larger house, able to seat all the cell leaders from that section. Pastor Hong meets that new area's middle management section leader, and they speak briefly. Soon he begins a monthly sectional service, held in the section leader's home for all the cell leaders and any willing participants from that section. Since there are eighteen sections in his subdistrict, Pastor Hong conducts eighteen of these meetings each month.

Musical strains of "There Is Power in the Blood" fill the room as we join to sing the beloved hymn. Then Pastor Hong leads everyone in concert prayer for specific needs.

In his sermon, Pastor Hong emphasizes the importance of persistent patience in ministering to others. Pastor Hong's text is James 5:10–11: "Brothers, as an example of patience in the face of suffering, take the prophets who spoke in the name of the Lord. As you know, we consider blessed those who have persevered. You have heard of Job's perseverance and have seen what the Lord finally brought about. The Lord is full of compassion and mercy."

After prayer, cell leaders bring in two tables of food. Lunch is festive as cell leaders share how God has been helping and blessing them. Two women describe a specific problem to Pastor Hong. He spends ten minutes counseling and praying with them.

The next homes are within walking distance. The section leader of that community then leads Pastor Hong, Senior Deaconess Kim, and me to nine more visits, all to church members in that area.

In one visit we hold a dedicatory blessing service over a new noodle restaurant before it opens for business. In three visits we pray for sick believers eager for healing. Two visits are to welcome members who have recently moved from other areas of the city. Pastor Hong then visits a tailor shop whose owner serves as men's cell group leader of that area and encourages the man in his Christian walk. We make another brief visit to a family struggling with limited finances.

By the fourteenth and final visit of the day, nine hours after our visitation began, my notebook has room for only one more entry:

"There is a continuous posture of ministry in this home visitation. Two things impress me. First, Pastor Hong flows with a quiet but powerful spiritual gift. In each visit he quickly discerns the heart of a situation. He knows the exact Scripture to turn to and what word or piece of wisdom to give. Most respond by nodding their heads. Some respond by crying. Others sigh in relief. All value his closing prayers of blessing.

"A second important thing is the layleaders who go with him. They hang on every word, often making notes and outlines of his short sermons. It is as if they plan to share with others what he has said. Sometimes he turns and gives instruction about how they are to follow up in ministering to a specific person. They take this entire process quite seriously. Perhaps because he takes his ministry so seriously."

The next morning Pastor Hong will send a copy of his report[2] with updated information to YFGC's extensive computer department, where clerks will enter the updated information into each family's file.

Staff Pastor's Typical Weekly Schedule

Monday—"Family Day"; the only full free day.

Tuesday—8:30 A.M. devotions with entire pastoral staff; spends remainder of the day (at least until 5:30 P.M.) in ministry visitation.

Wednesday—8:30 A.M. hour of prayer with staff pastors in his district office; spends remainder of the day in visitation unless he is one of a handful in the district office during the three worship services at 2:00, 5:00, and 7:00 P.M.

Thursday—8:30 A.M. hour of prayer with staff pastors in his district office; spends remainder of the day in visitation; at least one evening each week he visits until 8 or 9 P.M.with men who work late.

Friday—8:30 A.M.devotions with entire pastoral staff; spends remainder of the day (at least until 5:30 P.M.) in ministry visitation; usually tries to nap before going to the all-night prayer service.

Saturday—8:30 A.M. hour of prayer with staff pastors in his district office; spends remainder of the day in visitation unless he is one of a handful in the district office during two afternoon worship services.

Sunday—Expected to be in his district office from 7 A.M. to 9 P.M. He takes time to join one worship service and to eat. Otherwise he is in the district office to pray and counsel with people, especially between worship services.

Modeling Ministry

Modeling of ministry is paramount at YFGC. By the time a church has several thousand members, the senior pastor usually considers himself too busy to do home visitation. That is not the case with Dr. Cho. In 1980, when the church had a full-time pastoral staff of 150 and nearly 150,000 members, Dr. Cho still made home ministry visits one day a week. Even now, with membership climbing toward the one-million mark and his frequent ministry trips overseas, he still occasionally makes home visits.

When he speaks to his pastoral staff in joint weekly meetings, Dr. Cho frequently reminds the pastors to be grateful that they are not visiting during the earlier days of the church. "The people you visit now," Dr. Cho says, "sometimes bring you orange juice, and a few even serve you meals. But thirty years ago, when the church was under a tattered tent, the people we visited were very poor. They could not even afford soft drinks. All they brought me was a glass of water. Sometimes I would drink so much water through a day of home visitation that my stomach sounded like a sloshing pool when I walked."

This modeling of ministry does not stop with Dr. Cho. In most scheduled ministry visits, staff pastors take one or more layleaders with them. These layleaders then continue the ministry they see modeled before them. Most layleaders I talked with described their weekly ministry visits as their favorite time of the week.

A Homegrown Staff

This modeling has resulted in a largely homegrown staff. In one survey I found that most of YFGC's staff pastors were raised up from within the congregation.[3] These staff pastors, most former layleaders with careers, well understand the struggles of those they minister to.

Staff pastors must have graduated from either Bible school or seminary. Many now on the pastoral staff have completed theological training in the church's former three-year evening seminary, allowing them to remain at daytime jobs and serve the local church as layleaders while undergoing further training. Others graduated from the Korean Assemblies of God resident theological school. But in the words of one layleader: "Those are the ones we have to teach about ministry after they come on staff."

To be accepted on staff, each potential staff pastor must pass a series of three tests: a lengthy denominational written test, focusing on theological concerns; a preaching test, when a five-minute sermon is evaluated by both an ordained pastor and an elder; and a personal interview, held by a grouping of both ordained ministers and elders.

Three out of every five pastors on this homegrown staff are female, a consistent trend throughout the church's history. However, only with rare exceptions can a female be more than a licensed minister (better translated "evangelist" from Korean).[4]

Setting Goals

Careful attention to numeric goal setting began in the 1970s, and has continued. Dr. Cho requires that staff pastors set annual goals for the number of new members to be added that year in their areas, as well as the number of new cell groups. Annual goals are further broken into monthly goals. These numeric goals are to be both birthed and bathed in prayer. Goal setting is closely tied to staff accountability.[5] Because the staff pastor is active in goal setting, each layleader is also challenged to set prayerfully defined goals to the glory of God.

YFGC also found it best to rotate pastoral staff. One reason this is done is because some areas of ministry are noted for their difficulty. For example, there are distant areas in the city of Seoul that require lengthy drives or bus rides from the church. A staff pastor assigned to a distant area for two years will often be assigned to a near area the next two years. There are also areas noted for poverty and struggle. After being assigned to one of these areas for two years, that staff pastor will usually be assigned to a middle income area the next two years. Another result of this rotation is the prevention of staleness and personal kingdom-building. Every two years staff pastors know they will have a fresh start and an opportunity to build the kingdom of God in a different area. On occasion, if there are repeated complaints about a staff pastor, rotation will be made sooner than the two-year period. However, this rotation of staff pastors has not resulted in a sense of unsettledness in the cell groups or among the members, for layleadership is not rotated. Cell leaders, section leaders, deacons, deaconesses, and other layleadership—unless they move with their family to another location—remain in place. Every two years layleaders know they will join with different members of the pastoral staff. Now YFGC assigns each staff pastor to a place of ministry for a period of two years and rotates him to another area for the next two years. During those two years, that pastor focuses ministry and goals solely on his or her area. Evaluation of pastoral effectiveness and that area's growth (or lack of growth) is made annually.

The Importance of Prayer

Dr. Cho emphasizes the importance of prayer to his staff pastors, even going so far as to mandate that each one pray for three hours a day. The first hour of each day begins with an hour of prayer, either in the office or at joint meetings.[6]

Staff pastors often talk of their continual prayer for God's wisdom. One pastor told me, "I get up in the early morning and pray two hours for layleaders, for the people I have visited, and for those I will visit. Each week I read two sermon books, looking for biblical solutions to people's problems." He paused and pointed to his head. "See this gray hair? I got this through the process of getting God's answers."

One fact observable by anyone who has spent time in Korea is that Korean pastors do pray more than most other ministers. Because of their direct personal involvement in people's lives through home visitation and the responsibility to model ministry to the dozens of layleaders working with them, Korean pastors have much to pray about.[7] This priority of prayer has a direct impact on the prayer lives of layleaders. It is not unusual when two layleaders first meet in the church to begin discussing their own prayer lives, then to talk about the prayer lives of their staff pastors who inspired them initially.

7

Outreach Fellowships

The main channel for YFGC's evangelism is the cell groups, taking the good news of the gospel into members' homes and communities. However, the increasing complexity of Korean society necessitated the creation of other kinds of evangelistic outreach. While the cell groups meet mainly on weekdays, such fellowships concentrate their planning meetings and evangelistic activities on Sundays. Because of a five-and-a-half- to six-day work week, Sunday is the only full day Korean Christians may have free.

An Emphasis of Reaching Out

"Outreach," says Dr. Cho, "is the life of the church. If you stop becoming involved in reaching out to others, then your strength of faith is drained. This is a basic secret to church growth."

This focus on outreach is best reflected in what has become a virtual motto of YFGC: "To live is for evangelism; to die is for the kingdom."[1] Outreach and evangelism are top priorities in decisions, activities, and attitudes. Effective evangelism leads agendas, and its presence or lack is a primary criterion for evaluation at least once a year.

Sunday is the day set apart for the Lord's work, a practice that has resulted in both spiritual growth for those involved and numerical growth for those whose lives are touched in Jesus' name. Many I spoke with also reminded me that Scripture is clear on the importance of the Sabbath Day: "Remember the Sabbath day by keeping it holy" (Exodus 20:8). Korean Christians consider Sunday the modern Sabbath, a day set apart for the work of the Lord. This view, combined with the church's priority of outreach and evangelism, gave birth to a practice some call "sacred Sunday, day of planning and evangelism."

Since Sunday is already the day most members come to church, every church office is fully staffed, often until seven that night. People find it more convenient to come to the offices between services to ask questions, receive ministry, and volunteer to work than at other times of the week. Others find Sunday the best day to meet to plan and implement evangelistic thrusts.

Many layleaders stay at the church, involved in one of a variety of activities, until late Sunday afternoon. Since many first-time visitors do not come until the 11:00 A.M. service or later, the 9:00 A.M. service is a favorite among layleaders who will stay throughout the day.

Each of YFGC's more than twenty outreach fellowships targets a different segment of society, offering a wide variety of activities. Whether a person has a heart to help struggling churches, is a professional actor looking for a way to spread the gospel through drama, or is concerned for the homeless and disabled, an outreach fellowship invites involvement.

Full Gospel Businessmen's Fellowship Union

On a cool day in April 1976, Dr. Cho was praying in his grotto at Prayer Mountain. As he prayed, God made one directive clear: He was to gather the church's businessmen to form a support base for its foreign and domestic programs. After he finished praying and left the grotto, Dr. Cho met a leading businessman of the church, Elder Sooung Kim. He was surprised to see the businessman at Prayer Mountain since he would normally have been at his office in the city, but told him about his time in prayer. Elder Kim was soon busy organizing the businessmen of the church.

One month later, a hundred businessmen attended the first monthly meeting of the Full Gospel Businessmen's Fellowship Union. The Union's activities expanded over the next three years to include prayer breakfasts, dinners, and scholarships to needy students. From 1980 to 1985 the Union established a variety of committees that later became outreach fellowships.

Domestic outreach fellowships now target diverse occupations and segments of society, including military personnel, entertainers, medical personnel, athletes, lawyers, transportation personnel, university and college professors, police personnel, prison inmates, industrial workers, churches in farming and fishing communities, beauty operators, and those socially ignored and derelict, such as prostitutes and the institutionalized insane. One such fellowship helps distribute Christian literature in Korea, and another helps support the church in television media. The four international outreach fellowships help support Korean missionaries in Asia, Europe, America, and former Communist countries.

Most of these fellowships have an office or room in the church's 260,000-square-foot World Mission Center, a short walk from the main sanctuary. After attending a Sunday morning worship service, many layleaders go to one of the nearly twenty mission outreach fellowships for a devotional service in an office in the World Missions Building. Later on, they break for lunch at a nearby restaurant, then either return to the church for volunteer work or go to a nearby location for related evangelistic ministry. Each fellowship helps the Full Gospel Businessmen's Fellowship Union fulfill its motto: "Outreach is our business. Our business is the Lord's business."

Farming and Fishing Communities Outreach Fellowship

Known to many as the king of the outreach ministries, the Farming and Fishing Communities Outreach Fellowship has been part of the church since 1982. Its nearly three hundred active members are divided into six teams, with up to three outreach teams traveling in rented buses each Sunday. Each one-way trip to churches in rural farming and fishing communities takes up to three hours.

What would it be like to participate in this fellowship? On an autumn Sunday, I decided to find out for myself. Our target outreach that day was Ahn Song, a rural farming community a two-hour drive from Seoul City. After we attended the nine o'clock

Sunday worship service, forty-seven of us packed into one bus and were on our way.

During the drive, Hangki Kim, the elder in charge of the Farming and Fishing Communities Outreach Fellowship, preached to us from 1 Corinthians 4:1–4 about being God's faithful servants. "God," he said, "looks for Christians who are faithful, even in minor commitments and promises. When we are faithful to God, He is faithful to bless and help us."

Elder Kim then told of a recent report from another church the fellowship had visited. The church had seventy church members before that visit from the fellowship, but it now had grown to two hundred. We rejoiced, then sang from our hymnbooks and prayed that God would be with us in Ahn Song and help many come to a saving relationship with Him.

Just as scheduled, two hours later our bus arrived at a small Methodist church; the female pastor who had invited the fellowship came out to greet us. Several men unloaded the sound system and musical instruments, and soon we sat down to box lunches.

After lunch, we gathered in the church (built in the day when there were separate entrances for women and men). We discussed our plans for outreach, then joined in prayer, asking God to also bless fellowship members at two other target locations that day.

After dividing into fifteen teams of two and three, we got back in the bus and were dropped off at strategic points throughout the farmland. We walked over dirt roads to each home, often a traditional Korean farmhouse with a thatched roof, and gave out printed invitations to come to a special service at the Methodist church that evening at five. Often we gave other Christian literature, all aimed at bringing the good news of the gospel to this community filled with nominal Buddhists and practicing animists. We spoke to each person we could about Jesus, careful to remember the locations of the receptive homes.

I was just a guest, but for a portion of the day I went with one team. I later joined the Methodist pastor to pray for a woman on her sixtieth birthday celebration. Several teams met back at the church by 4:30 to help set up for the service. Some teams went back to receptive homes and accompanied people to the service. By the time of the service, the small church was packed with nearly forty new people from the community, a few from the regular congregation, and members of our fellowship. Elder Kim gave a fiery evangelistic sermon and then asked those who wanted to receive Jesus as their personal Lord and Savior to raise their hands. Throughout the crowded church more than twenty teary-eyed newcomers raised their hands. Pastor Kim invited them to return to the church. New believers completed decision cards, given to the host church to do follow-up in the coming week.

We loaded the bus by seven in the evening, both joyful and exhausted. We sang and prayed most of our return trip, getting back to YFGC just as the last Sunday service was coming to a close. "This was our first time to visit that area," one team member said, "but I have a feeling we'll be back. We want to help that church grow even more."

After we returned, I talked with layleaders and learned how this fellowship receives invitations. The churches that ask teams to come range in denominational background; the only prerequisite is that the church be evangelical. Teams go to the same church up to twice a year, and stories of their lasting impact are frequent. Up to 250 people have come to the Lord in a single revival service.

Gabsun Cha, a deacon and long-standing member of the fellowship, told of a visit to Yondae Li Baptist Church, when only eight people regularly met under a vinyl tent. During the fellowship's first visit, twenty people were born again and became members of the fledgling church. On their second visit, two years later, they collected an offering for the purchase of a building; soon after, membership climbed to 200. By their third visit, two years later, 750 church members met in their own building.

This Farming and Fishing Communities Outreach Fellowship also gives monthly financial assistance to five hundred struggling rural churches. Funding for this effort comes from nearly three thousand supporting church members. One goal of the fellowship is to give monthly financial support to a thousand rural churches in farming and fishing communities throughout South Korea.

Telecasting Outreach Fellowship

Another way YFGC reaches unbelievers with the gospel is

through media. The Telecasting Outreach Fellowship works with Dr. Cho in financially supporting the televised broadcast of Sunday church services over seven Korean stations, reaching most of South Korea. This commitment to use media to spread the gospel is reflected throughout the church's fellowships.

Each Sunday after the 9:00 A.M. service, members of the Telecasting Outreach Fellowship meet for prayer and discussion. Future plans include connecting the main sanctuary in Seoul with the largest sanctuary at Prayer Mountain through a microwave system.

Police and Military Personnel Outreach Fellowships

By 1989 the combined Military and Police Outreach Fellowship found that ministry demands on them were too great, so they divided into two separate fellowships.

Following the eleven o'clock Sunday morning service, dozens of volunteers work at the Military Outreach Fellowship to bundle more than thirty thousand copies of Christian literature to be sent weekly to twenty-five hundred Korean military posts and locations throughout the country. "We don't just send Christian literature," explained Senior Deacon Chanho Chong; "we also hold services in military chapels and counsel those from the church who enter the military."

He continued, "Military service is compulsory for adult Korean males, and each year two hundred thousand young men enter the Army. This gives us an excellent opportunity to reach them with gospel literature, because a lonely soldier will read anything available. We have received hundreds of thank-you letters. It is important that these soldiers know Christ and arm their minds and hearts with the gospel, for they are the ones protecting the nation of South Korea. We encourage Christian officers to be free in sharing their faith and to maintain personal contact with military chaplains."

Dr. Cho is a popular speaker at large military gatherings, often speaking to thousands of soldiers and officers gathered expressly to hear him.

The Police Outreach Fellowship currently sends Christian literature—including the weekly church newspaper, monthly Christian magazine, audio sermon tapes, and Bibles—to 800 police stations. Elder Kyungshin Park reports that the more than 3,000 police stations are manned by 130,000 police personnel throughout South Korea. Future plans are to help those in the church's geographical districts pair with nearby police stations to help win the police officers to the Lord. Elder Park says, "The main headquarters for the Korean S.W.A.T. [Special Weapons and Tactics] teams are in Seoul. We provide pastors and teachers to minister in Sunday services held in the headquarters building. As a result, many S.W.A.T. team members have come to the Lord. Each Sunday at 11:00 A.M. we have a meeting with members of the Police Outreach Fellowship in our office. We know things happen when we pray together."

Entertainers' Outreach Fellowship

Nearly five hundred members belong to the Entertainers' Outreach Fellowship, which is divided into three departments: the Music Department for singers and musicians, the Drama Department for television actors, and the Dance Department for those involved in classical dancing and ballet. Members of this fellowship often work with Dr. Cho and other fellowships and church ministries to use their talents to draw people to the Lord. They perform dramas on Sunday afternoons in smaller church auditoriums, so believers can bring non-Christian friends to see the gospel enacted.

Kook Shin, a well-known actor on the MBC Television Network, visits prisons twice a month to perform biblical drama. He said, "I usually play the role of Jesus in our dramas. I particularly remember visiting Kwachon Prison. The first time we did a biblical drama there, only about a hundred prisoners attended. By the second visit there were nearly three hundred people, some carrying Bibles, others crying as we sang hymns. By our third visit, the prison hall was packed with six hundred people. That time we joined with the Police Outreach Fellowship and served food. During each visit, at least thirty people stood to receive Jesus as their personal Savior. I watched those prisoners' expressions change from bleak despair to bright faith in God."

Social Welfare Outreach Fellowship

Few domestic fellowships have the impact on the hurting as

the Social Welfare Outreach Fellowship. Established in 1980, this fellowship focuses its efforts on the outcasts of society: lepers, prostitutes, the homeless, and wives and mothers abandoned by their families. According to Deaconess Dongwha Lee, on a typical Sunday afternoon members divide into several groups and hold twenty-three services in government housing, nursing homes, hospitals, and facilities for the emotionally and physically dysfunctional. Members prepare for ministry by fasting and praying often in the days before and by gathering for a Sunday service in their office before being sent out.

While the somewhat related Prison Outreach Fellowship focuses its Sunday efforts on visiting inmates and giving them Bibles and Christian literature, the Social Welfare Outreach Fellowship provides financial help for abandoned children; it has also built three churches: one for catatonic patients, another for lepers, and a third for the deaf—all in different provinces of Korea. The deaf church that started with 7 now has a membership of 859.

International or Foreign Mission Fellowships

Outreach fellowships do not focus solely on South Korea. Each international mission fellowship aids evangelism in its target area, largely through support of Christian media and of the Korean missionaries sent out by the church's Missions Department. By January 1992, the Missions Department had sent out 353 missionaries, who had established 267 churches in 32 countries. The majority are Korean congregations.

Each international mission fellowship has its weekly devotional service in a separate room on Sunday morning at eleven. Many gather later on Sunday to prepare Christian literature for mailing to missionaries and others and to discuss planning details.

One goal of the Japan and Asia Mission Fellowship is to win ten million Japanese to Christ through support of Dr. Cho's Japan crusades, the televised Japanese program "Invitation to Happiness," the publication of Japanese Christian books, and the biweekly newspaper *Japanese Gospel Journal*. This fellowship also supports Korean missionaries and evangelistic efforts in Thailand, Malaysia, Taiwan, Singapore, the Philippines, and East Asia.

The spirit of partnership prevails in these fellowships. Support of Dr. Cho's Korean and English television programs is a focus of the America Mission Fellowship; Dr. Cho can be seen weekly on ten stations in America. This fellowship also sends Christian literature and aid to the 164 Korean pastors and wives who minister to Korean congregations in North America. They support broadcasts to reach thousands of Korean immigrants living in the South American countries of Brazil, Argentina, Paraguay, Bolivia, and Chile. YFGC has installed a ten-minute sermon telephone line that can be reached twenty-four hours a day. This highly effective outreach has also been installed in a hundred Korean churches on the American continents.

The Europe Mission Fellowship helps in the support of the thirty-one Korean pastors in Europe and helps in the production of audiovisual aids and broadcasting programs. It sponsors annual trips to the Holy Land as well as visits to missions locations in Europe.

The most recent international mission fellowship, established in 1985, was originally called the Communist Bloc Mission Fellowship. Since the political changes in former Communist countries, Elder Jongsuk Lee says that they have revised their motto "evangelizing the communist bloc countries of the world" to "evangelizing the northern countries of the world." This fellowship supports a wide range of activities to spread the gospel to those still confined in Communist countries, as well as those suffering in former Communist countries.

Several elders involved in the fellowship have already made many trips into mainland China. The fellowship assists fifty churches by sending financial support, shortwave radios, more than a thousand copies of the weekly church newspaper, Bibles, hymnals, and other Christian literature. The mission supports four Chinese-Korean missionaries inside mainland China, who teach Chinese church leaders in short-term programs. Its Mandarin Chinese language club totals over four hundred beginner and intermediate students.

The fellowship collects money to send clothes, food, and needed supplies to Christians in those lands. It also sponsors a Russian language club for beginners and weekly Sunday prayer meetings for the spread of the gospel in those countries and a ten-minute daily radio program with a sermon by Dr. Cho, which broadcasts throughout Communist North Korea.

Organization of the Outreach Fellowships

Throughout the fellowships YFGC has clear lines of communication and delegation of authority, but with much room for individual initiative. Although Dr. Cho initiated some fellowships and activities, many were suggested by layleaders.

And although most fellowships were begun by laypeople, all are run by laypeople. The Full Gospel Businessmen's Union, responsible for the development of more than twenty outreach fellowships representing thirty thousand participants, employs only two full-time staff pastors. The primary work of those staff pastors is to make ministry visits to members' homes and to businesses. Volunteer leaders run and operate the fellowships, with an occasional paid staff person in larger fellowships.

Funding for the outreach fellowships is provided solely through the voluntary giving of interested church members; funding for the Women's Fellowship, Senior Deaconesses' Fellowship, and the Senior Deacons' Fellowship is provided by the voluntary giving of layleaders. The church provides only space for an office or room for each fellowship and occasional preapproved announcements in the weekly bulletin.

Each new fellowship is initiated by either Dr. Cho or a contingent of elders—often businessmen in the Union—who then submit the suggestion to Dr. Cho. Since the church budget provides no monies to fund the fellowships, Dr. Cho appoints an elder known to motivate others to start a new fellowship.

New outreach fellowships are launched with a Sunday announcement of a special prayer meeting that week in the 2,000-seat Paul Chapel, one of several chapels throughout the church complex. Those who attend this designated prayer meeting are told of the proposed fellowship and invited to become supporting members, contributing on a monthly basis. Only a portion of supporting members actively participate in evangelization and volunteer activities on Sunday, with some giving financial support to up to three different fellowships. An estimated thirty thousand people give monthly financial support to the outreach fellowships.

The foundation of Christian relationships formed in these fellowships is not based on social interaction but on mutual ministry. Participants pray, worship, and join one another in study, outreach activities, and volunteer work.

A staff pastor told of overhearing a conversation in a restaurant near the church between two women who had not seen each other for a year. One woman, a former member of the church, had moved to another city and was visiting for the weekend. "You should have heard them talk," the staff pastor said. "They were so happy to see each other. They had both been involved with the Farming and Fishing Communities Outreach Fellowship. Each treasured memory was based in ministry—what had happened during a revival service at a particular church, the response of a woman they had visited, the time they had shared the gospel with a taxi driver. They talked and laughed for an hour. By the time they left, a precious relationship built on the foundation of ministry was renewed."

8

The Church's Doctrine

What does YFGC believe and teach that has affected so many thousands of lives for Jesus Christ? Dr. Cho is now known as one of the most powerful preachers of his day, credited with doctrine that has affected the lives of millions.

One reason for the continued interest in YFGC's doctrine is the strong spiritual dynamic present in its teaching and preaching. Whether one sits in a worship service, participates in a home cell group, or attends a Bible class at the church, there is a distinct sense that, as one man has said, "God is present among us."

Members explain, "All teaching at YFGC is bathed in prayer. When we pray in faith, God's Holy Spirit is free to work among us."

Life-Transforming Doctrine

One family grateful for the doctrine in Dr. Cho's preaching is the Choe family. Mr. Choe was a poor schoolteacher on Korea's Cheju Island. When his wife began having gynecological problems, all he could afford were simple over-the-counter remedies. But when her pain increased, he finally took her in for a medical examination.

Doctors diagnosed Mrs. Choe in the last stage of uterine cancer, which by then had even spread to her colon, and gave her no hope of recovery. Since he had no health insurance, the poor Mr.

Choe brought his wife home to die, hoping he and their children would be able to comfort her. She lay on the bed, her stomach badly swollen, in increasing agony.

Yoido Full Gospel Church's
Official Confession of Faith

I believe that the Word of God was written by the true and infallible inspiration of the Holy Spirit.

I believe that the three persons of the Holy Trinity, Father, Son, and Holy Spirit, work in unison.

I believe that the redeeming blood of Jesus Christ is the only source for the atonement of sin.

I believe that Jesus Christ rose from the dead, ascended into heaven, and will come again. After His reign of 1,000 years, a new heaven and earth will be created which will last forever.

I believe that everlasting life is prepared for those who believe in Jesus, while eternal punishment awaits unbelievers.

We of Yoido Full Gospel Church recite the Apostles' Creed whenever we meet for worship and believe that all its statements are true.[1]

Mr. Choe finally called their five children together and said, "Your mother is dying. I cannot stand to see her in such pain any longer. Stay with her while I go get an ambulance to take her to the hospital."

Too poor to even have a private telephone, Mr. Choe prepared to walk to a local hospital. Before he left, he went to the side of his wife's bed. Since they were Christians, they had often listened to Dr. Cho's sermons on the church's weekly radio program, sometimes recording them on audiotape. To get her mind off the pain, Mr. Choe grabbed one of the tapes and put it in the recorder to play. "I am going to get an ambulance to take you to the hospital," he told his suffering wife. "They can give you medicine, and you can at least die with less pain. Listen to this tape while I am away."

She grimaced with pain but listened to the sermon as best she could. On the tape Dr. Cho explained how the believer's body is a temple of the Holy Spirit but that our minds and wrong thinking can block Him from freely working in our lives. Near the end of his sermon, Dr. Cho seemed to be speaking directly to her: "You might be a good Christian, but up to this point you have been resisting the truth of divine healing. The God who healed yesterday also heals today. By His Holy Spirit, He dwells in you.

"God wants to heal you, but your unbelief and wrong thinking have been resisting Him. Why do you resist the truth of divine healing? Renew your mind with the truth of God's Word and receive your healing. Jesus Christ is the Great Physician."

Dr. Cho's words pierced Mrs. Choe's heart. "Oh, God," she prayed in broken sobs, "all these years I have been resisting You as my Healer. I thought that it was ridiculous to believe in a God who heals today. I am dying. I now confess that God the Healer lives within me. I surrender to You. I believe in Your healing power. Oh, God, I am desperate! Come now, touch and heal me! I believe! I surrender myself to You and to Your Holy Spirit!"

Suddenly she felt a warm sensation within her, like a surge of electricity. Hurriedly, she asked her perplexed children to help her to the bathroom.

When she came out of the bathroom, her stomach was flat, and her pain was gone. She sat down and began singing, then shouting, then crying. Her children gathered around her. When they realized that their mother had been healed, they also began to cry and shout.

Several minutes later, her husband arrived on their doorstep with the ambulance driver. When he heard the commotion inside, he thought his children were crying at his wife's death, so he and the ambulance driver kicked in the door. Then they stared in shock, for his wife sat smiling, a look of health radiating from her face. "What happened?" Mr. Choe asked his crying children. "Is she a ghost?"

"Mother was healed by the power of the Holy Spirit," one child blurted out. "While she was listening to Dr. Cho's sermon tape, the power of the Holy Spirit came and she was healed."

The driver of the ambulance surveyed the situation. He had heard the gospel before but had always been skeptical. But Mr. Choe had told him of his wife's situation, and he knew he was looking at a miracle. There in that humble home, the ambulance driver knelt down and gave his life to Jesus Christ.

Mrs. Choe continues to enjoy radiant health. Her husband

later quit his job and moved to Seoul so he could go to Bible college. He and his family eventually returned to Cheju Island, where they have started a church.[2]

Not all responses to the doctrine in Dr. Cho's preaching and in YFGC's teaching are as dramatic as that of the Choe family, but all touched by YFGC's ministry consider its doctrine both vital and life-transforming.

Elder Chulik Lee, a member in the church since it was located at Sodaemoon, explained that Christians in Korea were taught that after death, a believer would go to heaven. "But," said Elder Lee, "they were not taught that you can be blessed in this life. As I listened to Dr. Cho's teaching, I realized that the Lord wanted to bless me in this present life, as well as in the eternal life to come."

Before the church offered planned Bible studies for the cell groups, Elder Lee often taught on the blessing of salvation in his men's cell group. "It was important for those in my group," said Elder Lee, "to understand that although Jesus came primarily to bring forgiveness of sins, He is still interested in healing our physical bodies and in our financial situations. Several in my group were healed and they also prospered financially. But one must first exercise faith in God's Word."

Biblically Based Doctrine

Doctrine based on the Word of God has been foremost in teaching all ages at YFGC. In each worship service and home cell meeting, participants recite the Apostles' Creed. One fall I observed a children's cell group. Their lesson that day, complete with visual aids, was "Three Proofs for the Divinity of Jesus Christ." It is possible that these children, by the time they reach adulthood, will have had as much doctrine and systematic theology as a first-year seminary student.

The church's Education Division is staffed by more than twenty pastors having a minimum of a master of divinity degree. The division has developed written curriculum for children's Sunday school classes, as well as seven books used by home cell groups. It also staffs and prepares material for the Laymen's Bible School, which gives a systematic overview of the sixty-six books of the Bible in seventeen weeks, and the Laymen's

Bible College, a six-month course covering topics like systematic theology, biblical theology, the life of Christ, church history, the Holy Spirit, ministry, church life, and church liturgy. Members who desire more Bible knowledge can go to these twice-weekly classes or concentrated Sunday afternoon classes. A minimum charge for each course covers the cost of materials.

At any given time, nearly twenty-five hundred men and women are enrolled in the Laymen's Bible School, and about the same number in the Laymen's Bible College. The majority of those enrolled are cell group leaders wanting to learn more about the Scripture.

However, these adult students want to do more than simply learn about the Scripture; they also want to apply it in their everyday lives. I remember meeting one woman who had gone through both the Laymen's Bible School and the Laymen's Bible College. She was shy by nature, and before she took the courses had been quite reserved in sharing her faith. As she studied about the love and power of God, understood the reality of heaven and hell, and began to realize the importance of the Great Commission, she started to share her faith more freely with others. By the time she completed the Laymen's Bible College, she had personally led ten people to faith in Jesus Christ.

The Threefold Blessing of Salvation

Two terms heard frequently in the church are "the threefold blessing of salvation" and "the fivefold message of the gospel." Closely related, these terms trace the primary doctrines in preaching and teaching throughout YFGC's history.

In those early days when the church met beneath the tent, Dr. Cho began to ponder the words of 3 John 2 (the Korean version being similar to the King James Version): "Beloved, I wish above all things that thou mayest prosper and be in health, even as thy soul prospereth." In this verse John noted three blessings in salvation: spiritual blessings, material blessings, and the blessing of health. This verse forms the basis for the "threefold blessing of salvation."

The verse hinges on the phrase "even as thy soul prospereth." Jesus died for the believer's sins, giving him spiritual salvation. By believing in Jesus Christ, the Christian can live assured of eternal life and an abundant spiritual life in the present. According to Staff Pastor Myungku Shim, "If our spiritual lives grow, other aspects of our lives will be enriched. If the soul does not prosper, nothing else will genuinely prosper. The first priority in the believer's life must be his personal relationship with God."

The church teaches that the phrase "that thou mayest prosper" refers to prosperity in this life. Jesus offers the believer the blessing of prosperity—freedom and salvation from poverty—considered the second blessing of salvation.

The church further teaches that God is concerned with our physical health, "That thou mayest be in health." Jesus offers the believer healing, which is salvation from sickness (Isaiah 53:5; 1 Peter 2:24). Jesus paid the price for our healing at Calvary, the third blessing of salvation. But the blessing of salvation in any realm—spiritual, material, or physical—must be appropriated by faith in God's Word.

I talked with one staff pastor about his thoughts on the sick who are not healed when he prays. "I do not always know the reasons why some people are healed and others are not," he honestly explained. "It is our responsibility as pastors to make every effort to move people into a faith posture to believe God's Word and to receive healing. I encourage and do not condemn those who are not healed. I do know that most of the people who have been healed have been persistent, coming to every church service and prayer meeting possible, and even going to our church's prayer retreat, Prayer Mountain, on several occasions to pray and fast."

The Fivefold Message of the Gospel

During the early 1970s when there were not enough funds to complete the sanctuary on Yoido Island, Dr. Cho focused his prayers and thoughts on the cross of Jesus Christ. As Dr. Cho meditated on the Cross, he was greatly moved by the redeeming grace of Jesus. It was then that the Holy Spirit impressed him with the five facets of God's redemptive grace. By 1974 Dr. Cho began teaching the fivefold message of the gospel.

"Throughout my ministry," Dr. Cho once told me, "I have always struggled to preach the full meaning of the redemption of Jesus Christ. I want to give people hope, faith, and solutions to their problems. It is my purpose to preach the Lord Jesus Christ and His total work of redemption."

SALVATION

First and foremost in the fivefold message of the gospel is spiritual salvation. This salvation comes through repentance of sins and confession of Jesus Christ as one's Lord and Savior (see Acts 3:19; Romans 10:9–10), and includes both forgiveness of sins and a new identity as a child of God.

Prominent in the church is the mammoth wooden cross hung behind the central pulpit, easily seen by all who fill the gigantic sanctuary. And when the main sanctuary was enlarged in 1983, a 100-foot tower was constructed outside, near the front stairs. This modern steel sculpture symbolizes two hands praying, with a steel cross in between.

The cross of Jesus Christ is central to all doctrine that YFGC teaches and preaches. Rarely a sermon is delivered when Dr. Cho does not remind the congregation, "Jesus Christ is the same yesterday and today and forever" (Hebrews 13:8).

In the words of one member, "Without the cross of Jesus Christ, we would have nothing. But because of His death on the cross, God has given us all things in Jesus."

One Bible account Dr. Cho frequently mentions is when poisonous snakes were sent among the Israelites and many were bitten and died. Moses prayed for the people, and God instructed him to make a bronze snake and put it on a pole. All who looked on that bronze snake lived (Numbers 21:6–9). Centuries later, as Jesus was talking to Nicodemus, He declared, "Just as Moses lifted up the snake in the desert, so the Son of Man must be lifted up, that everyone who believes in him may have eternal life" (John 3:14–15).

The paramount principle in teaching and preaching, Dr. Cho asserts, is to lift up Jesus Christ. Jesus himself said, "But I, when I am lifted up from the earth, will draw all men to myself" (John 12:32). The goal of doctrine is to draw men and women into a deepening relationship with Jesus Christ.

At the conclusion of each sermon, those who want to receive Jesus as their personal Lord and Savior are asked to stand and repeat a sinner's prayer. All throughout the massive sanctuary people can be seen standing, some with tears flowing down their faces, others with solemn conviction. Blue decision cards are distributed, with completed cards returned in the offering bags; follow-up is as immediate as possible. On a typical Sunday, one elder estimated, between three hundred and five hundred decisions for Christ are made in this manner.

THE BAPTISM IN THE HOLY SPIRIT

The second aspect of the fivefold message of the gospel centers on the baptism in the Holy Spirit. It is only through the Holy Spirit that one can become born again (John 3:5); however, His role does not end with regeneration.

YFGC's official brochure states that the "believer can receive the baptism, the fullness, of the Spirit at the time of salvation or soon after salvation. All who receive the baptism in the Holy Spirit (Acts 2:4) receive power and are witnesses of Jesus Christ (Acts 1:8). In their lives they show forth the gifts and fruit of the Holy Spirit, bringing great glory to God."[3]

It is believed that the baptism in the Holy Spirit opens a new avenue for God to operate in the believer's life. This baptism gives the believer greater empowerment, as well as a new prayer language. When one "speaks in tongues," one is praying under God's guidance. Paul wrote, "I will pray with my Spirit, but I will also pray with my mind. . . . I thank God that I speak in tongues more than all of you. . . . Do not forbid speaking in tongues" (1 Corinthians 14:15,18,39).

In a survey conducted by Dr. Sunghoon Myung, 76 percent of the congregation believe that speaking in tongues is the outward evidence of the baptism in the Holy Spirit, and 63 percent speak in tongues in their daily prayer lives.[4]

Even though he had spoken in tongues once in Pusan, Yonggi Cho did not have much regard for the baptism in the Holy Spirit until he went to Bible school. He later said, "I knew something was missing in my life. Jashil Choi, my future coworker and mother-in-law, was the oldest student in the school. She came early to class for prayer. As she prayed, she spoke in a strange language. I laughed at her, 'Why do you speak that gibberish? Speak Korean to God!'"

She replied, "I have the fullness—the baptism—of the Holy

Spirit, and I speak in tongues. When I do, I receive great edification. When I speak in tongues, I have more spiritual power than you."

Each Saturday a group of students used to witness in a public park. Yonggi Cho would pound his drum, the group would sing, and all kinds of people gathered around. Many mocked them; others tried to argue with them. But in the midst of that, they preached.

Yonggi Cho considered himself more polished and capable than Jashil Choi. But even though he felt that he preached a wonderful theological message, not one person accepted Jesus.

Then Jashil Choi would preach. He considered her sermons poor and unorganized. "Just listening to her preach," he said, "I felt ashamed for her. But then I noticed that when she spoke, people listened. Suddenly, the whole place calmed. It was as if some strange wind began to gently blow. Those same people who mocked us would grow quiet, laugh, clap, and listen. When she gave an invitation for those who desired to become born again, people would come to be saved."

He shook his head. "I could not understand it. It seemed unfair of God. When I spoke, people argued with me; but when she spoke her poor message, they listened, laughed, cried, and got saved. Why? She was full of the Holy Spirit, surrendered to Him."

So Yonggi Cho watched her throughout Bible school. She could not compete with him academically, but evangelistically she surpassed him as well as all the other students.

Dr. Cho wanted to have that same kind of power. Before he graduated, he decided to get away to fast and pray, choosing Samgak Mountain in Seoul as a retreat. "Father God," he said, "You've got to give me this baptism in the Holy Spirit. Choi is forty-two years old. She is getting too old to be used effectively, but I am just twenty-two. She lived in sin in the world until she was forty. But You see me; I'm a fresh, young man. Why don't You give me the Holy Spirit? Otherwise, I will not go into the ministry."

He argued and insisted that way all night. Finally, he felt that his heart was completely empty. "It felt like a big vacuum," Dr. Cho related. "The next moment I felt the presence of the Holy Spirit. I knew that I had received the baptism of the Holy Spirit, and I, too, received my prayer language and began to speak freely in tongues.

"After that, when I preached, a holy hush seemed to fall on people and they listened intently to me. Many were convicted and came to salvation in the Lord Jesus Christ."

DIVINE HEALING

The third aspect of the fivefold message of the gospel focuses on divine healing and deliverance. Jesus devoted two-thirds of His ministry to healing the sick and casting out demons. Christ promised that "these signs will accompany those who believe: . . . they will place their hands on sick people, and they will get well" (Mark 16:17–18).

Since Jesus "took up our infirmities and carried our diseases" (Matthew 8:17), the church teaches that born-again believers have the duty and privilege of praying for the sick.

Dr. Cho never preaches without praying for the sick and teaches his members to pray for others to be healed. This is not a doctrine to be taken lightly. In one survey, seven out of ten members reported that they had at some time been physically healed. Six out of ten said that they have experienced the casting out of demons, or evil spirits, in prayer.[5]

The truth of divine healing became more real to me when I was a girl of eight. I had a dog named Happy, an attentive and playful golden cocker spaniel I loved to play with. But as Happy grew older, he began to lose his sight, and a white glaze covered his eyes. In the cold of winter, we brought Happy into the warmth of our small silver trailer, but it wasn't easy for him. My young heart would almost break as I watched Happy bang his head on furniture he could not see.

By that time I had learned to appreciate the young Cho. Once I had lost my English Bible in the church, and the next week he came to our house to give me a new illustrated English Bible with my name inscribed on the title page. When group pictures were taken at the church, I often posed sitting in his lap.

On one of his visits to our home, Mom told Cho of Happy's problem and my distress. I remember as the young Korean minister bent over, placed his hands on Happy's eyes, and prayed for my dog's sight. The next day there was no longer a white glaze over Happy's eyes. My dog and I played together joyfully that day, no longer hindered by Happy's blindness. And I had learned two important lessons: God is indeed a healing God, and He is concerned with every detail of our daily lives.

PROSPERITY AND BLESSING

The fourth portion of the fivefold message of the gospel deals with prosperity and material blessing. Prosperity is reflected in one of Dr. Cho's favorite verses: "Christ redeemed us from the curse of the law by becoming a curse for us . . . in order that the blessing given to Abraham might come to the Gentiles through Christ Jesus" (Galatians 3:13–14).

Dr. Cho repeatedly states that poverty is not a virtue. Persisting through poverty with the help of God is a virtue, but poverty itself is not. Poverty is a curse.

"Look at Abraham," Dr. Cho says. "He never starved. God blessed him so much that he had abundant silver and gold. Isaac inherited Abraham's blessings, and God added even more to him."

Dr. Cho continues, "Look at Jacob. He was also greatly blessed with prosperity. God called himself the God of Abraham, Isaac, and Jacob. If being prosperous is wrong, then Abraham, Isaac, and Jacob are the worst kind of Christians you could have. But they were God's chosen people."

Jesus promised to feed and clothe believers who first seek the kingdom of God and His righteousness (Matthew 6:25–33). When one lives for the glory of God in honesty and faithfulness, he will have enough abundance to pay his bills and to share with others (2 Corinthians 9:8). The goal of financial prosperity, Dr. Cho contends, is not to hoard possessions and security for oneself but rather to give for the expansion of God's kingdom.

Within the context of God's blessings, people at the church are taught to give and tithe. Members view financial giving as an act of faith in God's promise to provide for their needs. Printed on each tithing envelope are these words: "Bring the whole tithe into the storehouse, that there may be food in my house. Test me in this . . . and see if I will not throw open the floodgates of heaven and pour out so much blessing that you will not have room enough for it" (Malachi 3:10).

THE HOPE OF JESUS' SECOND COMING

Fifth in the fivefold message of the gospel is the blessed hope of the second coming of Jesus Christ. Only a select few saw Jesus' first coming (Luke 2:8–16), but His second coming will be seen by all people (Matthew 16:27; Philippians 2:10–11). Believers will attend the Marriage Supper of the Lamb (Revelation 19:9) and will reign with Christ for a thousand years (Revelation 20:1–5). After the Great White Throne Judgment, believers will live a glorious life forever with God in the new heaven and new earth (Revelation 21:1).

But hope for future blessing must never cloud the reality of the present work of the Kingdom. The last statement on the inside page of the church's brochure says: "YFGC believes that its greatest mission is to preach the gospel of Christ to the whole world, teaching the Fivefold Message of the Gospel and the Threefold Blessing of Salvation."[6]

The church's doctrine has not been without its critics. In earlier days fellow ministers criticized Dr. Cho for his zealous preaching on divine healing and prosperity. Most criticized has been his preaching on dreams and visions, one way the Holy Spirit deals with believers. This criticism is largely based on misunderstanding the source of dreams and visions and the process by which they come to pass.

"Visions and dreams," contends Dr. Cho, "are often the language of the Holy Spirit in helping us form goals and direct our lives. I usually receive guidance by reading Scripture. I believe in faithfully studying the Bible. There are times when a passage seems to leap at me in a new way and burn into my heart. Then I know God wants me to act on it.

"God also uses the desires He has planted in our hearts, as well as circumstances, to guide us. But these must line up with God's Word. When God gives us a vision or dream, that becomes a goal that He wants us to target."

Criticism has not stopped Dr. Cho from continuing to preach the "full" gospel, nor has it stopped people from coming to hear him.

9

The Sermons

I was curious. My friend Lee Weeder had been away from her native Korea for twenty-seven years. Lee was an educated woman, a licensed clinical social worker who served as a professional counselor in inner-city Washington, D.C. She had been married to an American man for twenty years and well understood both the American and Korean cultures. So when we attended a worship service at YFGC for her first time during my 1989 research trip, I watched Lee's reactions.

Lee was amazed. She could hardly believe the sense of unity and partnership she saw, for one Korean proverb states that where there are two Koreans there are at least three opinions. Her dark eyes danced as she turned to me and said: "This has to be a work of God for all these Koreans to come to the same church and have such unity. I can only believe this because I have seen it for myself."

Yet what amazed her most was Dr. Cho's preaching. "I first thought Dr. Cho would preach on some unique or unusual story in the Bible," she said, "but his sermons were simple and direct. When he spoke, even though I was sitting in a large, crowded sanctuary, I felt as if he were speaking God's words just to me."

Later, when I asked ten random YFGC members why they thought the church has grown so large, nine mentioned Dr. Cho's preaching. Staff Pastor Sungjin Bin told me, "Dr. Cho's sermons give vision, hope, and clear direction. He speaks out not only against sin, but also in support of the practical aspects of Scripture that we can use in our daily lives."

Some people ride the city bus for ninety minutes each way just to come to church. When I questioned why they don't go to one of the other five thousand churches around Seoul closer to home, most said, "Because when I hear Dr. Cho preach, God uses his sermons to talk to me."

One Dramatic Lesson

Yonggi Cho did not always preach such powerful and relevant sermons. Perhaps the most dramatic lesson he learned about preaching came from the days when he visited the homes of members and the unchurched as pastor of the fledgling tent church. "I learned," he once told me, "that it was best to forget what I had learned in Bible school about writing sermons. When I wrote my sermons from what I learned in textbooks, they did not relate to people's daily lives."

One family in the tent church's poor and simple community was particularly well-known. The husband had been an alcoholic for ten years and could not keep a job. His wife was always sick with either heart or stomach pains. Their ten children stole whatever they could or shined shoes to provide their father with money for alcohol.

Cho determined to go and preach to them his usual message of heaven and hell. He arrived at the door of their small room and knocked. The wife appeared, a look of dejection on her face. "Lady," he began, "I am pastor of a church in your community. I want you to know that Jesus Christ died for your sins and offers you eternal life. Repent of your sins, believe in Jesus Christ, and go to heaven."

She responded with a sneer. "Listen, Preacher, you go to heaven. I'm not going to heaven."

"Why not?" he asked. "Jesus Christ died for your sins. He is now in heaven and has prepared a beautiful place there for you. Jesus offers you heaven free of charge. He has already paid the price."

She spoke back angrily, "If you have such a beautiful heaven, why don't you give me a part of that heaven right now on earth? We need food, we need clothing, we need a proper home, we need money to educate our children. We are dying, suffering every moment. If God is not concerned about our lives this day, how can you be sure that God will give us heaven in the future? Why don't you give me a bit of heaven now so I can believe in the heaven of the future?"

Cho replied, "But if you don't believe in Jesus Christ, you are going to go to hell and burn eternally."

The woman's anger mounted. "Hell? We are already living in hell! My husband is an alcoholic. We fight and argue every day. None of my ten children goes to school. They shine shoes and are pickpockets and thieves. We have no food to eat, and we all live in one small room. Bedbugs crawl on us while we sleep. We are already living in hell. Hell could not be worse than this!" With that, the women slammed the door in his face.

His usual message of heaven and hell was not going to touch this family. The young Yonggi Cho went back to the tent church and knelt in prayer.

Shift from Tradition to Relevance

Cho determined to read the Scriptures in a new light. His schooled approach was not effective. As he read, he noted that Jesus forgave sins, healed the sick, cast out devils, cleansed lepers, raised the dead, fed the multitudes, and preached. Often Jesus dealt first with immediate needs and then spoke of spiritual things.

Who would not then listen to the good news of the kingdom of heaven? With new resolve, he returned to see the woman. She opened the door and exclaimed, "You again? I told you to go! I'm not listening to you anymore!"

"Please listen," Dr. Cho pleaded. "I am not going to preach about heaven and hell today. I have good news to tell you."

"Good news?" she sneered. "Even the government cannot give good news to us. What kind of good news do you have?"

He quickly replied, "Your husband is no longer going to be an alcoholic. He is going to become a new person who will love you and your children. You are going to be healed from your stomach pain and heart problems. Your children are going to go to school and be educated. And you are going to have a good place to live."

She laughed, "You are some liar!"

"No," Cho asserted, "I am telling you the truth. When you come to the Lord Jesus Christ, when you surrender your life to Him, He is going to give you all these things."

Her eyes danced with fleeting hope. She asked, "Where is your church?"

"Follow me," he instructed.

She left her house to walk beside him, and they finally arrived at the worn tent church. She asked, "Where's your church?"

"This is it," he replied.

She looked at the bedraggled tent structure and burst into laughter. Then she looked straight at him, "You say you are preaching good news, but you are the one who needs that news. You are no better off than I am." She continued laughing.

The young minister was inwardly frightened, but he maintained, "What you say is true. I, too, need Jesus' good news. I am in great need of the help of God. So why don't we together believe in this good God who is going to meet your need and my need?"

Yonggi Cho's honesty touched her. "Yes," she replied, now solemn, "I will believe with you. No one else has given me any hope before now."

So each day she joined Cho, and together they prayed for God to meet their needs. Within three months her husband was miraculously free from alcoholism. He became born again and started attending church. His few friends then banded together and got him a job. With the money he brought home, they began sending their children to school. They finally saved enough money to buy land and build a house. Two of their sons later became ordained ministers.

Preaching to the Multitude

Yonggi Cho's preaching would never be the same. Through the years he developed into what many call the most relevant and listened-to preacher in all South Korea. Now seven times each Sunday thousands of people gather in long lines, waiting to hear Dr. Cho preach in the next worship service. He preaches to people in need, much like the poverty-stricken woman with the alcoholic husband and ten children.

Consider the example of Jesus. Multitudes thronged to see our

Lord. The people came because of felt needs and desires. Some came to see miracles, others to feed on the loaves and fish Jesus provided (John 6:26). Still others wanted to hear His "teaching with authority" (Matthew 7:28–29). Yet, even though the multitudes came for their own personal needs and curiosity, Jesus was faithful to minister to them.

Those at YFGC with the most marked felt needs—the multitudes—are most likely to come to the weekend Saturday and Sunday services. Dr. Cho's repeated sermon on those days covers subjects relating to current needs and daily living, with three to five practical points. Two vital segments are central after Dr. Cho preaches on these weekend services: the invitation to those who want to become Christians and prayer for the sick to be healed.

Preaching to the Disciples

Jesus' ministry was not limited to the multitudes; He was also encircled by disciples—first by the Twelve, and, later, by the Seventy (Mark 3:14; Luke 10:1). Many of these disciples had once been only part of the crowd themselves, until they obediently responded to Jesus' call to deeper commitment.

Once that poor woman with ten children and the alcoholic husband that Cho had reached out to had come to Christ, she did not remain only a part of the multitude. Her commitment to the Lord and His Word deepened and she became a disciple.

At YFGC, the three Wednesday services are attended mainly by the layleaders of the church—the committed disciples—so Dr. Cho gives expository sermons on Wednesday, often covering one Bible chapter at a time. In fact, the home cell group curriculum is based on years of these sermons, which gives verse-by-verse explanations and illustrations.

The primary disciples at the church are the pastoral staff. Most YFGC staff pastors were born again or healed under Dr. Cho's ministry. Many attended the church's former evening seminary classes, and they counsel and preach the same message as Dr. Cho. One member commented, "No matter which staff pastor I listen to, it seems as if I am hearing the same voice proclaim God's Word."

Dr. Cho's sermons are now direct and compact, his weekend

sermons typically half an hour long—a good length for the attention span of visitors brought by members of the congregation and a necessity for seven back-to-back services each Sunday. Either his Saturday sermon or his 9:00 A.M. Sunday sermon is taped and televised throughout South Korea, except in Seoul. This is one of the many ways that Dr. Cho preaches in partnership with the congregation. YFGC members know visitors will consistently hear interesting, biblically based sermons on relevant topics. One man gave me his perspective: "I come to church because I am a partner with Dr. Cho. As often as possible, I bring an unbeliever with me to church so he can hear Dr. Cho clearly preach the Word of God. As I do my part in bringing others to church, God also does His part. I have already seen many of my friends and neighbors come to the Lord this way."

Sermon Preparation

How does Yonggi Cho prepare such powerful sermons that touch lives for God? When asked about his first priority in ministry of the Word, Dr. Cho immediately answers, "Prayer."

Cho typically starts his day with one to two hours of prayer. After lunch he prays half an hour more. In the evening he prays at least an hour. Before his Sunday sermons, Dr. Cho usually prays three consecutive hours. Before speaking at a crusade in a largely non-Christian country, he has been known to pray for seven hours. It is Dr. Cho's practice to "minister to the Lord" in prayer before "ministering to the people" in preaching.

One of the most cherished spots at Prayer Mountain, the church's prayer retreat, is Dr. Cho's personal prayer grotto. He spends hours on his knees in prayer many Fridays and Saturdays, preparing to preach the next day, a key to the strong anointing felt by those who hear his messages.

Members of the congregation make it a daily practice to pray for Dr. Cho and his upcoming sermon, the pastoral staff, and those in leadership. Many YFGC families also pray for their pastor, his preaching, and their church during daily family devotions.

Perhaps the greatest prayer warriors of the church are the more than four thousand senior deaconesses, women over the age of fifty, credited by many as the prayer backbone of the con-

Weekly Worship Service Schedule

SundaySpeaker
6:30 A.M. Staff pastor or guest
9:00 A.M. Dr. Cho
11:00 A.M. Dr. Cho
1:00 P.M. Dr. Cho
3:00 P.M. Video of Dr. Cho's latest sermon
5:00 P.M. Video of Dr. Cho's latest sermon
7:00 P.M. Staff pastor or guest

Wednesday
2:00 P.M. Dr. Cho
5:00 P.M. Staff pastor or guest
7:00 P.M. Video of Dr. Cho's latest sermon

Saturday
2:00 P.M. Dr. Cho
5:00 P.M. Video of Dr. Cho's latest sermon

Each evening
10 P.M. to 4 A.M. Staff pastor or guest (sometimes Dr. Cho on Friday nights)

gregation. Most of these women consistently pray two hours each day. Oaksohn Kim, former president of the Senior Deaconesses' Fellowship, told me that she prays daily for each member of the Cho family, asking God to protect and bless each one, as well as for Dr. Cho's preaching and ministry.

Relevant, Hope-filled, and Easy-to-Understand Sermons

Many of Dr. Cho's sermon topics are gleaned from his years spent in home visitation, when he learned the specific concerns and problems people daily contend with. "I never preach on a topic I have thought up by myself," he explains. "When I prepare a sermon, I ask God to help me know the mind of the Holy Spirit, who inspired the Word of God and ministers to people at their point of need."

The topics of Dr. Cho's sermons are as diverse as "How to Have a Happy Family Life," "How to Have Success and Integrity in Business," "Overcoming Difficulty," and "How to Experience

God Daily." But no matter what topic he chooses, he clearly shows how God's Word guides and relates to people's daily lives.

Since his days in Bible school, Dr. Cho remains an avid student of God's Word. Once he chooses a sermon topic, he prayerfully reads and studies all the applicable Bible passages he can find. His personal library is filled with more than a dozen versions of the Bible, several concordances, many commentaries, and hundreds of Christian books, especially those written by renowned men and women of faith.

After studying God's Word, Dr. Cho prepares a simple sermon outline with key points. "I then meditate on each point in the outline," he explains. "As I meditate and pray, the Holy Spirit gives me fresh understanding in what God's Word means and how each truth can best be taught and illustrated to meet the needs of the thousands who will hear the sermon." These outlines contain practical guidelines to help one know how to apply God's Word in everyday life.

The Bible, considered God's inerrant Word, is foundational to all Cho's preaching. His topical sermons usually refer to four or five Bible passages, with two-thirds of the passages from the New Testament and one-third from the Old Testament.

In earlier years, before his sermons were recorded, most members brought notebooks to each worship service, carefully taking notes of the sermon. Later, they would share its message with those they ministered to and visited. Today, the church tapes his sermons, and the rush at the end of each service for copies is almost more than the three YFGC bookstores can handle.

Preaching with Authority

Those who listen to his sermons, like my friend Lee Weeder, often remark on the note of authority with which he preaches. "It is as if Dr. Cho knows he has heard God speak, and then proclaims that Word to us," one man commented. "God has used Dr. Cho's sermons to speak to me so many times that I would not miss coming to church unless I was near death. And then I would be doubly sure to come, because I would want him to pray for my healing."

Dr. Cho's preaching with authority does not mean that he preaches condemnation. On the contrary, his preaching is positive and filled with hope. In his sermons he often refers to the believer's identity in Christ Jesus and the importance of faith in God to daily living.

Dr. Cho tells a classic story of why the tone of a sermon should be positive. There were four men trying to get a stubborn donkey to move from sitting in the middle of a road. One man threw rocks at the donkey, but it wouldn't budge. The second man got behind the donkey to push it, but it didn't move. The third man got the reins of the donkey and tried to pull it, but it still didn't move. Then the fourth man got a carrot and held it ten feet in front of the donkey. The donkey got up and walked forward.

Dr. Cho often tells visiting pastors, "Condemnation does not bring cure. It only dampens spirits. Christ condemned only self-righteous hypocrites. We are not to preach from Mt. Sinai, where thunder and lightning flashed as people were condemned. Instead, we are to preach from the pulpit of Mount Calvary, giving people faith and hope in the cross and in the finished work of Jesus Christ. Look at people through Jesus' eyes of hope."

On another occasion, Dr. Cho related the same concept of hope while expressing his attitude toward dealing with sin: "If I were a medical doctor, would I kill a patient to destroy an infectious germ? Some may think so, but a good medical doctor would never do that. He would nurse the sick person and warn him of the nature of that germ. Sin is a germ in the system of the sinner. But the sinner should not be destroyed, but rather the sin in his life—the germ. The sinner is not our enemy."

Having Goals in Preaching

Dr. Cho's preaching has three goals: "to help people come to a saving relationship with Jesus Christ, to help people succeed in life, and to motivate the believer to serve God and his fellowman."

Those who come to hear Dr. Cho preach—from executive businessmen to factory workers—are quick to tell how their lives have become more successful after applying the principles they heard in Dr. Cho's sermons. One businessman I talked with related how his business had more than doubled since he started coming to the church and listening to Dr. Cho's sermons, while another told how he had been on the verge of suicide and now had a prosperous company.

Dr. Cho's sermons are both simple and memorable, laced with illustrations from Scripture and everyday life, including current events. One spring there was a great deal of construction before heavy rains. Dr. Cho preached a sermon on brokenness, explaining how difficulty can benefit the believer: "Some wonder why God allows any difficulty in this life. Think of the weather. Sunshine is wonderful, but if all you have is sunshine, the ground becomes dry, and drought soon sets in. Rain is also needed. You, too, must go through wet and stormy days if you are to bear fruit."

He also said, "Or think of a building. Before they build up, they dig down. When your mind and heart are shaken by difficulties, it is broken down, expanded, and surrendered. God purposely allows trials and tribulations to expand us to receive more of Him."

In another illustration, he said, "Without death, you will not have the success of resurrection. So when trials and difficulty come, shout! If you persist in Jesus' strength, you will have success and resurrection. On the other side of brokenness is blessing."

In a sermon on the nature of God, Dr. Cho told of a young barber who asked him, "How could a loving God allow sickness, wars, and misery in this world?" Dr. Cho responded by asking him to walk down the street. As they strolled down the sidewalk, an old man walked toward them. His hair was uncombed, his clothes ragged, and his beard tattered. Then Dr. Cho turned to the young barber and asked, "How can you be a barber and allow that man to walk around the streets of this city looking like that? It's a disgrace."

The barber grew defensive. "How can I take responsibility for that man if he does not come into my shop to have his hair cut and his beard trimmed? I have all the equipment to clean him up, but he has to come into the shop first."

Dr. Cho emphasized, "God has already provided the answers and solutions to all man's needs in Jesus Christ. But if man does not come into God's storehouse of salvation, man has chosen to live in his state of misery."[1]

Illustrations Worth Noting

Dr. Cho's illustrations are relevant to the Korean culture, as well as reflecting biblical values on evangelism and Christ's work on the cross. In a sermon on hope in Jesus Christ, he told of witnessing to a young woman who responded, "I will come to church when I am ready to die. I am too great a sinner and am ashamed to come to church."

Public bathhouses are popular throughout South Korea, starting in the days when there was little indoor plumbing. Even now many women make a practice of going to a ladies bathhouse once or twice a week. Dr. Cho asked the young woman, "Do you go to the public bath when you are all clean?"

She replied, "No, I go when I am dirty, so I can get clean."

"The church is a spiritual bathhouse," Dr. Cho explained. "Only spiritually dirty people are welcome. Clean people don't need to come to church."

"I've never thought of church that way. I always thought that just good people could go to church."

"No," Dr. Cho retorted. "Dirty sinners are welcome! You do not know the time and hour you will die. Don't wait to come to church. Church is where sinners are to come!"

"All right," she agreed, "then I will come to church."

In another sermon on building godly relationships, he stressed the importance of love and commitment. To illustrate, he told the story of a young pregnant woman who fled south alone during the Korean War. When she came to the outskirts of a town, she felt the pangs of childbirth and had to stop beneath a bridge to deliver her baby. The winter winds grew bitter cold, so she wrapped her clothes and body around the infant, letting her warmth keep her baby boy alive.

Early the next morning, as an American missionary couple were driving on that same small bridge, the wife thought she heard the sound of a baby crying. The husband stopped the car and went to investigate. He discovered a naked woman frozen to death, clutching a small bundle. Only because of her clothes and care had her baby boy barely survived.

After burying the woman in a grave on the mountainside, the couple took the boy home and raised him as their own son. Years later, he became curious and asked them about his birth mother and father. Finally, his adoptive parents told him the story. The young man then searched until he found his birth mother's grave. Taking off his clothes, he placed them on her grave and wet the ground with his tears.

"We see in the birth mother of this story," Dr. Cho emphasized, "a reflection of Jesus Christ. He loved, and was committed to, all who came to Him, despite their doubts and weaknesses. He healed the hurting, encouraged the brokenhearted, fed the hungry, and gave solution to the searching. Then with His death, He gave us all His very self. Christ's example of love and commitment to us shows how we are to be committed to others."[2]

Public prayer is also made for Dr. Cho. Each layleader who prays in the first portion of the worship service prays for Dr. Cho, often at two or three points during his prayer, specifically asking God to anoint his message that day. The congregation usually joins in at this point, together speaking a hearty amen.

Early in the service the text of the sermon is read to the congregation. When Dr. Cho comes to the central pulpit, he does not begin preaching immediately. He prepares the hearts of those present to receive God's Word, first by leading the congregation in two to five minutes of concert prayer and then by leading in the church anthem and one or two gospel choruses.

Prayer of Application

Dr. Cho concludes his sermons with prayer. Often he will say, "You must do more than apply the principles of the Bible to have an effective life—you must first receive Jesus Christ as your personal Savior, for it is Jesus who will help you to overcome."

After leading in a prayer of salvation those who wish to receive Christ, Dr. Cho then guides the congregation in a sometimes lengthy prayer of application. This time of concert prayer is the most fervent prayer of the entire service, as people ask God's help to apply to their daily lives the truths they have just heard. Most give a portion of this time to repentance, whether of sinful attitude or action.

After this time, Dr. Cho prays for the sick, often telling of healings he senses God is bringing about. He then leads the congregation in repeating key phrases or thoughts from his sermon to further apply the truth of that sermon to their hearts.

Following a sermon entitled "Four Failure Factors in Christian Work" (which included pride, greed, immoral life-style, and selfishness), Dr. Cho had the congregation repeat the following after him:

I am a new creature in Christ Jesus. My pride has gone. My greed has gone. I no longer live an immoral life-style. Behold, I am a new person in Christ Jesus. I now live a new life with new hope. I now have new victory with new blessing.

The impact of Cho's dependence on the Holy Spirit is evident. Visitors often remark on the simplicity of his sermons, then add, "But it was powerful. I could feel God's presence when Dr. Cho spoke."

As a child Yonggi Cho was shy. His father called him "a sensitive chord on a violin." Added to his negative view of himself, he was born in Korea's southernmost city, Pusan, and spoke with a heavy southern Korean accent—not always appreciated in other parts of the country. Because of the Korean War, he had limited formal education.[3] The prospects of his becoming a great preacher were slim, but through the years he learned to depend on the Holy Spirit. Dr. Cho now emphasizes, "The Holy Spirit is in each believer. Recognize the Holy Spirit. Welcome Him. Appreciate Him. Depend upon Him."

And when Dr. Cho explains to visiting ministers his dependence on the Holy Spirit, he says, "Before I preach a sermon, I say, 'Dear Spirit of the Lord, Senior Partner, let's go! I am just Your junior partner. I depend on You.' It is through my dependence on the Holy Spirit that I have confidence and power. Without my Senior Partner, I can do nothing."

10

The Worship Services

What would it be like to attend a worship service at the world's largest church? Come with me for a Sunday worship service and see for yourself.

As we begin our journey together, it is nearly eleven o'clock on a Sunday morning, and the sun is bouncing off the Han River surrounding Yoido Island. Already a surging tide of people have streamed into YFGC's massive round sanctuary to attend Sunday's third worship service. Thousands go up stairways and thousands more climb circular ramps to the highest balconies. You and I watch as others from an earlier service flow down central stairs to crowd into city buses lining a wide boulevard entry.

As we walk toward a side entrance, the sound of incoming buses to the left of the mammoth sanctuary catches our attention. Each Sunday, cell group members charter dozens of rental buses to bring themselves and non-Christian friends to one of YFGC's worship services.

The worship service will begin shortly, so we hurry up a circular ramp. Latecomers walk to one of the church's overflow chapels where they view the service on closed circuit TV monitors.[1] At the same time, in scattered locations throughout the sprawling city of Seoul, others are filling one of YFGC's nearly dozen regional sanctuaries, soon to watch a video of yesterday's early Saturday service on giant screens. Together these facilities accommodate nearly sixty thousand for a single worship service.

We quickly find a seat on the third pew of the balcony, a section designated for foreigners. We pick up headphones that will transmit a simultaneous English translation, piped in from nearby booths.

We look down on a sea of people already praying, most moving back and forth as they silently petition God. It's quiet during this designated time of silent prayer, but we can sense both the power and the peace of God. Dr. Cho walks onto the upper level of the platform and kneels to pray. This quiet act signals the profound importance of prayer to the congregation; nothing is done without first asking God's guidance and direction.

A senior staff pastor walks to the far left of three pulpits on the upper level of the platform, opens the worship service by reading a psalm, and then leads the congregation in a time of silent meditation on God's Word. We join with the congregation in singing the Doxology, reciting the Apostles' Creed, and singing the chorus of a familiar hymn. Then an appointed elder stands at the far right pulpit and prays a lengthy prayer. Two topics of the elder's prayer are always the same: the welfare and blessing on the nation of Korea, the pastoral staff and other church leaders, and the congregation.

After the elder's prayer, the senior staff pastor once more enters the left pulpit and reads the text for the upcoming sermon. Today it is Matthew 24:14—"This gospel of the kingdom will be preached in the whole world as a testimony to all nations, and then the end will come."

The choir, wearing cream-colored robes, then stands, and a hundred voices sing the selection for this service, a joyful aria from Handel's *Messiah*. At the end of their anthem, Dr. Cho rises to the central pulpit. His dark brown eyes sweep over the expanse of faces. "Please stand," he begins, "and let us now pray for three things: for the welfare of our nation, for the leadership and outreaches of our church, and for our families."

The reverent hush awakens to a roar of concert prayer. Soon we hear nearly thirty-five thousand voices blend in a mounting crescendo of prayer. For the next two minutes we continue to pray and petition. The volume continues to rise. Suddenly Dr. Cho rings a bell. A hush promptly falls on the congregation.

Dr. Cho then gives the fifth prayer in the meeting. (There will be five more occasions of prayer before the end of the service.) He asks God to bless and anoint his sermon.

Although several elements, such as singing the Doxology and reciting the Apostles' Creed, are present in thousands of other churches, at YFGC these activities are applied with fervency and Christ-centeredness; they are not empty rituals but meaningful worship, a continuous reinforcement of biblical belief. Most of these elements have been in YFGC's worship services since the church began.

At each service, strategically stationed deacons and deaconesses distribute weekly church bulletins, printed with that service's sequence and listing the specific staff pastors and layleaders involved.[2]

All who participate feel the impact of these worship services. One man said: "Every time I leave a worship service, I know that I have heard God speak to me, and I know that God has heard my prayers. Coming here each Sunday is not a duty, but a precious delight."

Several key principles of worship at YFGC are evident in every service.

Spiritual Nurture of Children and Youth

YFGC sets important priorities in each worship service. Although not seen during the adult services, one priority is to provide spiritual nurture for the children and youth.

During the worship service, children's Sunday school classes meet in auditoriums, classrooms, stairwells, hallways, and on sidewalks—using every space available. On this warm summer Sunday morning, brightly dressed children even congregate in classes scattered across unused portions of the church's guarded parking lot for their own time of prayer and learning about God and His Word.

Children who participate experience the reality of God in their lives. Oakki Whang had severe stomach pains when she was in first grade. Doctors could do little for her, and medication was expensive. By sixth grade she thought her discomfort would be permanent. Then a friend invited her to attend one of YFGC's Sunday school classes. The lesson she heard that day struck a deep chord of truth in her young heart, so Oakki committed her life to Jesus Christ. That day Oakki was also healed. She now attends a Sunday school class for middle school students. "I'm healthy now!" she exclaims. "But more important, I know God loves me."

Each Sunday, nearly thirty-two hundred trained teachers instruct more than twenty thousand children and youth in large and small groups on the main church grounds and in nearly twenty[3] satellite Sunday schools in outlying communities. These Sunday school classes provide for the children of church members as well as the children of unbelievers.

Middle school and high school youth meet in separate auditoriums for their worship services, then break into small groups for discussion and prayer. Each Sunday afternoon at one o'clock, university students meet at the church's Antioch Chapel for their Christ's Ambassadors mission service and then divide into nearly a hundred groups for concentrated Bible study. Home cell groups for children and youth meet on weekdays.

There is no adult Sunday school. Rather, adults are provided further teaching through the cell groups that meet in private homes and offices, and through YFGC's Education Division, with weekday and weekend Bible classes at the church campus.

Priority of Evangelism

One woman who has benefited from YFGC's worship services is Guisoon Chang. When we met at a cell group meeting, Guisoon was happy and joyful. "But," she told me, "I haven't always been this way."

Six years earlier, Guisoon was desperate. Her husband's business was bankrupt, and several doctors diagnosed her with three different maladies—a heart problem and two related nervous disorders. Her body ached all over. Guisoon was in such pain that she determined to commit suicide by taking sleeping pills.

Just when she was about to take the pills, a Christian from YFGC stopped by to see her. "If you believe in the Lord Jesus Christ," her Christian acquaintance told her, "all will go well in your life." Guisoon went to one of YFGC's worship services with her Christian friend. She enjoyed the choir and congregational singing but was surprised when everyone stood and prayed aloud. Guisoon had never sensed such unified spiritual power. Dr. Cho even had to ring a bell on the central pulpit to signal the congregation to stop praying.

After he preached, Dr. Cho prayed for the sick. Then he added, "Through the Holy Spirit I sense there is a woman here whose husband's business has failed and whose finances have come to an end. God wants you to know that He is going to make all things well. Would that person please stand up?"

Guisoon stood up. She was surprised that anyone would know her situation and that God would care. That day she decided to receive Jesus Christ as her Lord and Savior, and her pain instantly lifted.

In the weeks that followed, Guisoon attended all the worship services she could and made it a practice to attend the all-night prayer meeting once a week. She also fasted breakfast a hundred days to pray for her husband's finances. Within three months her husband's business had reversed. Within three years her husband and five children had become Christians.

"I try to never miss participating in worship service on Sunday and Wednesday," Guisoon told me. "God blesses me each time I attend. That's why I try to bring others with me."

Guisoon and many others would quickly tell you that YFGC gives evangelism top priority, even in its worship services. Dr. Cho often compares YFGC's home cell groups to a net, encircling unbelievers with God's love before bringing them into the church. "Sinners are brought to the church as the members of the cell groups invite friends and neighbors," explains Dr. Cho. "It is then my responsibility to preach the gospel of salvation in such a way as to catch those sinners and bring them into the kingdom of God. Both the cell groups and the preaching of salvation in need-meeting worship services are needed for the system to be fully effective."

Near the start of the service, an elder prays that "all Koreans, from both the south and north, come to a saving relationship with Jesus Christ." Dr. Cho's sermons are laced with testimonies of people who have been born again, telling how salvation has transformed their lives. The culmination of a worship service comes at the conclusion of Dr. Cho's sermon when he invites all who want to receive Jesus Christ as their Lord and Savior to stand and repeat a sinner's prayer after him.

At this point I have often seen prayerful cell group members nudge their guest visitors, as if to say, "Now you can publicly declare your faith in Jesus Christ. Now it's time—stand up."

Excellence in Song and Music

Since church members often bring guest visitors, the twelve YFGC adult choirs and two orchestras view their role as important in the evangelism process. "I was skeptical when my Christian friend first brought me to YFGC," one convert said, "but when the choir sang, it was really good. Somehow the choir's excellent and spirited singing helped me see that this was genuine. I came three more times before I accepted Jesus Christ. I continue to attend and enjoy the choir."

In each worship service, a hundred robed choir members fill the large choir loft to the left of the main sanctuary's platform, a constant reminder of the priority YFGC gives to music. Nearly fifteen-hundred choir members serve in one of twelve adult choirs; a different choir sings at each of the twelve weekly worship services. Choir names are taken from the Bible: the Jerusalem, Hosanna, Bethany, and Nazareth choirs among the most long-standing.

Two orchestras alternate and accompany these choirs. More than a hundred members compose the Hallelujah and Gloria orchestras, many being gifted Christians who also play their instruments in Seoul's Philharmonic Orchestra.

These choirs and orchestras strive for excellence. Choir members are carefully screened in auditions in which they must read music and sing. Then they must go through an apprenticeship. Every week each choir has two practices, usually before or after the service in which they minister and before the Friday all-night prayer meeting.

Choirs minister in several ways during worship services. In each service, the choir sings one special song, ranging from contemporary favorites to sacred classics. There are also at least three times when the choir sings softly in the background as the congregation prays: during the beginning silent prayer, after the elder's prayer, and at the end of the service, following the benediction. The choir also joins the congregation in singing hymns and choruses. Solos are extremely rare, with emphasis on congregational participation.

Christians in Korea buy their own hymnbooks and bring them to church with their Bibles. YFGC members bring two hymnbooks, one traditional and the other filled with gospel choruses, many written by Dr. Cho and his wife, Grace. In addition to two hymn selections, the congregation sings three songs in every worship service: the Doxology, the church anthem, and the closing Lord's Prayer. The church anthem is based on 3 John 2— "Beloved, I wish above all things that thou mayest prosper and be in health, even as thy soul prospereth" (KJV).

This emphasis on participation has been beneficial. Most members also use their hymnbooks and sing gospel choruses during their daily personal devotions. Values established during worship services continue to have their impact on members' daily lives.

Consistent Giving

According to choir conductor Hosung Kim, "There are only two times in a worship service when we minister to God: first, when we sing our praises to Him, and then when we respond to His Word by giving our tithes and offerings to His kingdom. The rest of the service, God ministers to us through the words of the sermon and through prayers for salvation and healing. Even when we pray, we ask God for something. How wonderful that twice during a worship service, we can minister to Him!"

Members look on financial giving as a privilege, part of their worship to God. The offering follows the sermon, for it is a response in gratitude for God's Word.

Testimonies of tithing benefits abound at the church. When I met businessman Ghisig Chung, he was quick to tell me how he started tithing soon after he became a Christian, at that time giving the monthly equivalent of $150. His salary increased each year after that point, tripling in three years. He now not only gives a monthly tithe of $450, but has tithed as much as $15,000 after making a large contract.

There are three basic types of financial giving during YFGC worship services: tithes, pledges, and freewill offerings. The most popular freewill offering is called a Thanks Offering, given either in anticipation of a future blessing or in gratitude for a past blessing. The amount inserted in a white Thanks Offering envelope is determined by the giver.

There is also a wide variety of pledges at YFGC, the two most common being a missions pledge and a building fund pledge.

Missions pledges are used to fund the many missionaries YFGC has sent out to foreign lands. Members make their missions pledges at the first of the year and pay their desired amount in specially marked missions envelopes each month. Whenever a new building, such as a regional sanctuary, is to be built, members make a pledge and insert money in specially marked envelopes once a month until they have paid the full amount of the pledge. Members can either insert pledge envelopes in one of the many wooden receptacles around the church facilities or give at the offering time.

Tithing envelopes, as well as other pledge envelopes, are sorted alphabetically by family name in racks lining the walls of a long hallway leading to the main sanctuary. Members tithe once a month, usually on Communion Sunday, since salaries in Korea are typically paid monthly.[4]

Before the offering is received, a senior deacon stands at the center pulpit on the lower platform and prays. The purpose of this prayer is to prepare hearts to give and to thank God for His blessings. For example, in one service I attended, Senior Deacon Yongou Pak ended his brief prayer with the words, "Thank You, Lord, for using the sermon today to remind us of Your great love. Your loving kindness, oh Lord, is more than we can comprehend. Now we give our tithes and offerings to You, to thank You for Your bountiful provisions. Please receive our offering now, we ask, and bless us for what we are about to give."

Sixty uniformly clad deacons and deaconesses with maroon bags then take the offering in about four minutes. The first two minutes, the choir softly sings as the congregation prays and the offering bags are passed. Before placing any envelope in an offering bag, believers quietly pray, asking God to bless both the gift and the giver.

During the last minute of the offering, the presiding senior staff pastor—a role rotated among the twenty-three district staff pastors—stands at the pulpit on the far left and makes major announcements of church news and upcoming events. This is the only time during the service when announcements are made. Dr. Cho then rises to the central pulpit. By this time, the deacons and deaconesses have placed the offering bags on tables at the foot of the platform. Before these bags are taken to a security room, one bag is given to Dr. Cho, who inserts his tithe and offering in that bag, showing his own value of giving to the congregation, and prays once more over the offering, often ending this prayer with, "Please receive our tithes and offerings as acceptable gifts in Your sight. Use this money for the growth of Your kingdom. Open now Your window of heaven, we ask, and bless us."[5]

Fervent Prayer

Prayer is a repeated practice in all worship services. Including the benediction, there are five scheduled times for prayer in a worship service.

However, this does not include the preacher's prayers before the sermon or the three prayers after the sermon (the sinner's prayer, the prayer of application, and the prayer for healing), or the singing of the Lord's Prayer at the close of the service. In the typical ninety-minute weekend worship service there are at least eight occasions for various types of prayer, taking a minimum of fifteen minutes of service time. The longest worship services are on monthly Communion Sunday, when up to thirty minutes are taken in as many as fourteen occasions for prayer.

Even before the service begins, the people are praying. It is the practice among most Christians in Korea not to talk with others when they first sit down, but to pray to God. When questioned why they do this, most respond, "Because the Bible says 'pray continually' and 'give thanks in all things'" (1 Thessalonians 5:17–18).

Each worship service begins with silent prayer, as the congregation meditates on the psalm or Scripture passage just read by the presiding senior staff pastor. This is also a prayer of preparation.

Several principles guide the prayer times in YFGC worship services. Importance is placed on properly modeling prayer for the congregation. In every service three people minister from the main sanctuary's upper platform: Dr. Cho or the designated preacher, the presiding senior staff pastor, and an elder. Before each sits in his chair on the platform, he kneels to pray. These quiet acts are a silent but powerful modeling of the necessity of prayer.

The modeling of prayer is not limited to clergy. There are two prayers modeled by layleaders in each service: the elder's prayer before the choir sings and the senior deacon's prayer before the offering. The nearly five hundred elders rotate to lead this prayer, one in every service for each of the twelve weekly services. The same is true of the nearly twelve hundred senior deacons who rotate to make the offertory prayer.

Prayer by two layleaders in each service has two effects. First, it gives greater visibility to YFGC's layleaders. More importantly, it signals that prayer is not just an activity for the clergy but part of every believer's privilege.

Another guiding principle in prayer times is that the people are not just to listen to others pray but are to actively participate in prayer, even during the worship services.

The greatest times the congregation participates in prayer are during two periods of concert prayer. One occasion begins before the sermon, after Dr. Cho shares one to five prayer topics. Everyone stands and prays aloud for these concerns, as well as any personal needs. In unison the congregation, like the musical instruments in an orchestra, pray aloud to God in agreement for the concerns mentioned. These are intense times of fervent prayer. First-time visitors often bristle at the surrounding noise, but the sense of unified spiritual power overcomes the strangeness, and soon most participate with enjoyment.

Many visitors have likened concert prayer to the sound of rushing waters. Others compare it to the sense one would have had at Pentecost. When I ask staff pastors why they practice concert prayer, they say that it reflects the Early Church's practice when they were confronted with a problem. They "raised their voices together in prayer to God" (Acts 4:24). Others refer to Matthew 18:19: "If two of you on earth agree about anything you ask for, it will be done for you." Concert prayer is now commonly practiced in most Korean churches.

PRAYER FOR OTHER LANDS

A constant topic for the first concert prayer is the needs of those in other lands. In 1992, nearly seven thousand people outside Korea wrote Dr. Cho with specific prayer requests. These requests from people around the world are translated and sent to Prayer Mountain, the church's prayer retreat. The original requests are then placed in a large clear plastic tray that rests on a table to the right of the central pulpit at the church. Before Dr. Cho preaches, he mentions this tray, and soon the congregation is praying beyond its own borders.

Another focus in this first concert prayer is the missionaries the church sends, as well as current events in other lands. Prayer is also made for Dr. Cho's upcoming trip to minister overseas. During this time, Dr. Cho frequently guides the congregation to pray for America, for as he says, "Without their intervention in the Korean War, we could not pray in freedom as we do today."

Prayer for those in other lands has extended the vision of many members and helped them to develop a corporate sense of mission to take the gospel to the uttermost parts of the world. I remember meeting one young man who had grown up in YFGC and was then a member of YFGC's University Fellowship. He proudly told me that he was studying Mandarin Chinese and thought one day he might be a missionary to mainland China. "After all," he added, "we've prayed for China many times in our worship services."

PRAYER FOR HEALING

The church believes that sickness has both natural and supernatural causes. During prayer for healing, Dr. Cho instructs, "If you are physically sick, place your hand on the area that needs healing. If you have a problem or have been wounded in life, place your hand over your heart." All across the sanctuary, people place their hands on their bodies and over their hearts. During this prayer for the sick to be healed, Dr. Cho also prays against the demonic forces causing sickness, casting them out in the name of Jesus.

Often after this prayer, Dr. Cho senses specific healings that have taken place. He then mentions the particular characteristics of a person's problem or sickness. If a person's circumstance is described, the person stands, often with hands raised in praise to God. This sense that a particular healing has taken place is linked with the gift of the Spirit termed the "word of knowledge" (KJV) in 1 Corinthians 12:8.

Members are quick to share testimonies of results of this prayer for the sick. Healings range from the disappearance of terminal cancers to the alleviation of arthritic pain. Sometimes these healings occur instantly during the service, and other times they are gradual.

Typical is the story of Inja Kim, a middle-aged woman with a visible skin rash on her hands and feet. Inja had come with a member of the church to a Sunday service. Near the conclusion of that service, Dr. Cho said there was a woman with a skin rash and that God was healing her. When Dr. Cho asked that woman to stand, Inja quickly stood to her feet.

Inja looked at her hands and feet, and the two-year rash immediately disappeared, never to return. Within a month, her husband's thyroid condition was healed. She is now an enthusiastic believer who serves as a women's home cell group leader. In her first year as a cell leader, Inja and others who joined her led sixty people to Jesus Christ. The secret to her evangelism, Inja states, "is to tell others what Jesus has done in my life."

PRAYER OF BENEDICTION

Worship services close as the congregation stands to sing the Lord's Prayer, singing diminuendos and crescendos to the final phrase—"for thine is the kingdom, and the power, and the glory, for ever. Amen." Visitors comment that this is the most moving portion of the service.

Outside the sanctuary, several thousand people are waiting to enter the next service. Seoul has added extra public buses during scheduled worship services, but no one wants to leave early, not even to miss the bumps and jostles of the departing crowd. The departing prayer of blessing has not yet been given.

Dr. Cho stretches out his arms and gives the closing benediction: "Now may the abundant grace of our Lord Jesus Christ, the everlasting love of our Heavenly Father, and the fellowship of the Holy Spirit flow in every area of your life. May God protect and guide you until we meet together once again. Amen."

A strong sense of God's presence permeates the sanctuary. The choir sings softly, while those standing pray once more. Then the choir grows silent. The service is over and the rush to leave begins. Another YFGC worship service has come to a close. People leave refreshed, sensing that they have been in the presence of God and His people, impressed with the vibrant worship services of the world's largest church.

SEQUENCE OR OF EVENTS IN MOST YFGC WORSHIP SERVICES

Event or activity	Person, if any, responsible
Silent prayer*	During this preservice time, people enter reverently and whisper their prayers to God.
Reading of psalm or other Scripture passage, followed by silent prayer of meditation	Presiding senior staff pastor (rotated among YFGC's 23 senior district staff pastors)
Doxology	Congregation stands to sing
The Apostles' Creed	Congregation recites in unison
Hymn selection	Sung by congregation
Prayer	Presiding layelder (rotated among YFGC's 500 lay-elders)
Reading of Scripture for sermon text	Presiding senior staff pastor
Choir selection	Presiding choir
Sermon (begun and ended with prayer, including "concert prayer"*)	Dr. Cho or presiding preacher: a senior staff pastor or guest minister
Invitation and prayer of salvation for those who want to receive Jesus Christ*	Dr. Cho or presiding preacher
Prayer of application*	Congregation ("concert prayer")
Prayer for the sick*	Dr. Cho or presiding preacher
Hymn selection	Congregation
Prayer for the offering	Presiding senior deacon (rotated among the more than 2,300 senior deacons)
Announcements*	Presiding senior staff pastor
Singing of the Lord's Prayer	Congregation
Prayer of benediction	Dr. Cho or presiding preacher

Before the congregation leaves, most spend a few moments in concert prayer as the choir sings softly in the background.

*These activities are not printed on the church bulletin but are still a part of the usual sequence of YFGC's worship services.

The Sodaemoon church with its last addition, 1966.

Yonggi Cho and John Hurston, 1968, broadcasting one of the first radio programs from the church.

Deacon Pak, Yonggi Cho, and John Hurston with bundles of clothes for flood victims in Seoul, 1963.

A subdistrict pastor intercedes for a need.

A wall of tithing envelopes at YFGC.

A subdistrict pastor points out the most evangelistic group on the chart.

Dr. Cho recognizes and congratulates an evangelistic section leader.

Yoido Full Gospel Church, 1980.

Dr. Cho speaks to his congregation during a recent annual missions convention.

Karen Hurston and Grace
Cho, 1990.

Dr. Cho commends John Hurston as the executive director of Church
Growth International at a celebration of the hundredth seminar, 1981.

Small Group Discussion

From the Introduction

1. Briefly share what you have heard or know about Yonggi Cho or YFGC.

2. Reread the many activities of YFGC observed by the visiting American minister (p. 13). If you had seen these activities yourself, what might have been your comment?

3. The Introduction names five parallels between YFGC and current circumstances in America. To which needs mentioned are you most concerned that your church or small group respond? What other parallels come to mind?

4. Share why you think it will be worth your time to read the remainder of this book.

5. Suppose someone should ask you, "What are the Christians of YFGC doing that others aren't?" With what you know or could imagine at this point, list two ways you might respond to this question. Add to this list as you continue reading.

From Chapter 1: The Early Years

1. South Korea had great need when the church began. Does America have great need? How would you describe the need now for us?

2. A prominent theme in the church's history has been the importance of partnership—first and foremost, obedient partnership with God. One way to express partnership in the Old

Testament was through covenant. Who were some of God's famous partners in the Old Testament? Look at Genesis 15:18; 26:24–25; 28:10–15; Exodus 3:1–10; 19:3–6.

3. Read Matthew 3:1–3 and Luke 8:1–3; 10:1–2 to identify some of the partners in Jesus' ministry. Christians are also partners with one another. Identify some partners of Paul's ministry in Acts 13:46 and Romans 16:3.

4. Name at least two people with whom you sense God has called you as a partner (consider your pastor, church leaders, small-group leader, Christian friends). What is one thing you can do this coming week to be a more effective partner?

5. Throughout the history of the church, thousands of people have been physically healed. What did Jesus say and do in Luke 4:16–21 and in verses 38–40? What truth does Hebrews 13:8 present? Have you or anyone you know ever been healed?

6. Another theme in the church's history is that desperate needs call for desperate prayer. When the church began under a tent, times and people were desperate. Why is it that many people do not turn to God until they are in such need?

7. Recall one time when you were desperate and turned to God. How did He respond?

8. Do you know anyone who has a desperate need, whether family, physical, emotional, financial, or spiritual? Have you been praying persistently for that person? If that person is born again, what would be a good word or Scripture verse of encouragement to share?

9. If the person you know of in desperate need is not born again, have you lovingly and clearly shared the message of the gospel with that person? Have you invited that person to church or to your small group? Name one thing you can do or share with that person this week.

10. God does bring the right person at the right time and place. Read Mordecai's words in Esther 4:12–14. Is there any situation now in which you are God's person in God's time and place? End your group time in prayer for one another, that you may be obedient to God's purposes in your lives.

From Chapter 2: The Ministry of Prayer

1. Read Jesus' parable in Luke 18:1–8. What does Jesus teach about prayer and the nature of God in this parable?

2. Why do you think it is important to pray with faith-filled reverence? Do you treat your church as a holy place of prayer?

3. Have you ever gone to an early-morning or all-night prayer meeting? If so, how did it impress you? If not, how could you participate in one?

4. Notice that YFGC never has a service with just prayer alone but usually near the beginning has the preaching of God's Word. Why do you think that is?

5. Is the spirit realm a reality in your life and thinking? How does prayer help the Christian in his ongoing battle with Satan? Read Ephesians 6:10–18.

6. Read four passages linked with the baptism in the Holy Spirit: Acts 2:1–4; 8:14–17; 10:44–46; 9:1–7. Share two things you notice from these passages.

7. Two areas of impurity mentioned in this chapter were unforgiveness and disobedience. Share one area of past impurity that hindered your praying with a pure heart and tell what you did to overcome it.

8. Is there something you are presently praying for that you sense you need to pray for specifically?

9. Think of the situations and people you have been praying for. What is one way you could "put feet to your prayers" this coming week?

10. Consider people or circumstances you have prayed for in the past. Describe one answer to prayer you have experienced.

11. Think of a person or a situation now in need of your prayer. Spend several minutes in prayer for that specific person or situation.

From Chapter 3: International Prayer Mountain

1. Do you have a place like Prayer Mountain where you can get away from daily distractions and draw nearer to God in prayer? If so, what has that place meant to you?

2. Most Korean Christians, like Jashil Choi, pray loudly and verbally—especially when there is a pressing need. Think over your own experience. How would you compare times when you prayed silently to times when you prayed aloud?

3. Review the main reasons people go to Prayer Mountain. How do you think such reasons would be different in your church or your small group?

4. One expectation of those who visit Prayer Mountain is that they will attend all four daily services. What advantage would this have?

5. Why do you think it would be important to have a pastoral staff at Prayer Mountain?

6. Describe one benefit of combining fasting with prayer. Do you think God would have you fast? When and for how long?

7. How could the concept of Prayer Mountain be adapted to your church or your small group?

From Chapter 4: The Ministry of Layleaders

1. Of the various ways the church encourages layleaders, which way do you think would be the most meaningful to you?

2. Perspective changes our value of ministry. In your service or ministry to your small group or in your church, do you see what you do as your "assignment from heaven"? How would that perspective change your attitude and actions?

3. Layleaders of YFGC give top priority to evangelism. What about you? On a scale of 1 for very little to 10 for a great deal, how would you rate yourself in evangelism?

4. How did Yunhyung Yu respond when a Christian stopped attending church and her cell group (p. 65)? Do you know anyone who has dropped out of your small group or church? Read Luke 15:3–7. How do you think God would have you respond?

5. Reread Changki Song's advice to a group leader (p. 66). Which part of his suggestion do you most need to hear? Why?

6. Why do you think it is important for layleaders to have visibility during worship services?

7. Give one or two reasons you think the section leader is considered so important in YFGC.

8. Before anyone is appointed as an elder, he has spent years ministering to others. What difference do you think this would make in his attitude and decision making?

From Chapter 5: Home Cell Groups

1. Consider your pastor: Have you neglected any area of responsibility or ministry (even in terms of praying for him) that has resulted in a heavier load on him or her? What do you think God would have you do about this?

2. Dr. Cho knew that God had directed him to release layleaders to start weekly home meetings. What were some of the problems he encountered?

3. When the men of the church rebuffed Dr. Cho's plan, Cho felt God directing him to use women in leadership. Consider the American culture: What people are often overlooked for leadership potential but have the time to minister to others? Could these people be used more in leadership or ministry in your group or your church?

4. Consider your involvement with small groups. Briefly share how your involvement with a small group has made a positive impact on your life.

5. Develop a list of reasons why it is important that cell groups be vehicles of God's miracle power.

6. A frequently voiced concept in the groups is: "Find a need and meet it. Find a problem and solve it. Find a sick person and pray in faith for his healing." How would application of this concept affect your small group?

7. Have you ever made a home ministry visit? What are some things you might do during a ministry visit? Do you know someone who could benefit from such a visit?

8. Briefly share an experience when you were instrumental in bringing someone to a saving relationship with Jesus Christ or to a church worship service. If you have not done either, briefly share why.

9. Have you ever identified target-unbelievers to reach for Jesus, and set goals? If so, what happened?

10. If a piece of Christian literature made an impact on you when you were an unbeliever, share that with the group. What kind of Christian literature might interest an unbeliever?

11. When you were an unbeliever, did a Christian take the time to establish a caring relationship with you? Explore some ways you might establish caring relationships with specific unbelievers.

12. Why do you think that visitation and care are important after someone comes to the Lord?

From Chapter 6: The Ministry of the Pastoral Staff

1. Which portion of the pattern of home ministry visits seems most significant to you?

2. How is ministry visitation different from participation in a small group? Where does ministry visitation now fit into your group or church?

3. Have you personally made a ministry visit to someone in your group or church? If so, did you learn anything generally about visitation in that process?

4. Develop a plan for home visitation to those who are participating in your group. Try to make a ministry visit (perhaps with another person) to someone in your group or church before the next meeting.

5. Name two ways home visitation can be of benefit to the person or family visited.

6. What benefits do you think would result from an approach such as the Grand Home Visitation to those in your small group or in your church?

7. Is there an unbeliever or unchurched person you might influence through a caring visit?

8. Why do you think the modeling of ministry is important?

9. How could a homegrown staff perhaps better minister than a professional staff? Discuss the advantages and disadvantages of a homegrown staff.

10. Goals—birthed and bathed by prayer—are vital to YFGC staff pastors and layleaders. How many people do you think God would have you lead to a saving relationship with Him during the next twelve months? The next three months? What specific steps do you think God would have you take to reach that goal?

11. How many people do you think God would have your small group lead to a saving relationship with Him during the next twelve months? The next three months? What specific steps do you think God would have you take to reach that goal?

12. Is your prayer life influencing anyone else?

From Chapter 7: Outreach Fellowships

1. What are some differences between what you do on Sundays after the worship services and what many members at YFGC do?

2. In an average week, how much time do you give to God through ministry in your local church? What does this show about your values? How do you think God might have you change this?

3. Consider the number of hours in a typical week that you or your small group spends in some form of Christian ministry. Should this be changed?

4. Think back on your own relationships. How many of your own relationships are built on a foundation of ministry? Do you think it makes any difference in the quality of your relationships?

5. Read 1 John 3:17–18. What application could these words have in a local church? In your small group? In your life?

6. Do you think the catchphrase "To live is for evangelism, to die is for the kingdom" could be said of your life? Why or why not?

7. Read Matthew 28:18–20. Discuss how you and your small group can give more priority to outreach.

8. If you could establish any type of outreach, what would it be? Whom would you target? How would you do evangelism? How would you show God's love in practical ways? What finances would you need and how could they be raised? How many people would you need to start?

9. Could you do such an outreach with your small group or in your local church with your pastor's blessing?

From Chapter 8: The Church's Doctrine

1. What doctrine or teaching has most changed or transformed your life?

2. Why do you think it would be important for Bible-based doctrine to be taught to all ages?

3. Give brief overviews of the threefold blessing of salvation and the fivefold message of the gospel. Which aspects of this teaching do you consider most needed in your life?

4. Read the account of the bronze serpent in Numbers 21:4–9 and its application in John 3:14–16. How should this principle apply in your life?

5. What is the role of the Holy Spirit in your life? Do you desire to be more yielded to the Holy Spirit? What could you do about it?

6. Have you or anyone you know been physically healed? Have you ever prayed for someone else to be healed?

7. When you give your tithe or offering to God, do you view

that as an act of faith in God's promise or provision? What does Matthew 6:25–33 mean to you?

8. Do you spend time anticipating Jesus' second coming? How do you think your hope in Jesus' second coming should affect your Christian life?

9. What are some ways God has given guidance to your life?

10. Have you ever been criticized for believing something in the Bible? How did you respond?

11. What difference do you think it would make to bathe all teaching in prayer? Spend time praying for God's help to lift up the cross of Christ more consistently in your life and to be more yielded to God's Word and His Holy Spirit.

From Chapter 9: The Sermons

1. Consider a sermon your pastor preached or a teaching in your small group that has affected your life. Briefly share what that sermon or teaching was and why it made an impact on you.

2. Read about the multitude in John 6:26 and Matthew 7:28–29. Now read about the attitude of committed disciples in John 6:67–68. How would you contrast the attitudes and needs of these two groups?

3. Are you only part of the multitude or are you a disciple? Why? What is one thing you could do this week to deepen your commitment to the Lord and His church?

4. Because members of YFGC's congregation feel they are partners with Dr. Cho, they often bring unbelieving friends and acquaintances with them to hear his sermons. Do you often invite (and bring) unbelievers to your church or to your small group? If not, why? Who is one person you could bring next week to your church or small group?

5. What are the principles Dr. Cho uses to prepare a sermon? Why do you think prayer is so important to his sermon preparation? How do you think that influences his preaching?

6. Is the Holy Spirit your Senior Partner? Read John 16:7–13 and Ephesians 4:29–32. How should you respond to the truth in these passages?

7. What is one reason you think Dr. Cho closes his sermons with a prayer of application?

8. Spend some time in prayer, first to apply the truths you

have learned and then to learn how you can be a better partner with your pastor or small-group leader. Also pray for an unbeliever you plan to bring to an upcoming church service or small-group meeting.

From Chapter 10: The Worship Services

1. One man called YFGC's worship services "a precious delight." Give one reason you think he said that.

2. In your small-group meeting, do you aim for a personal encounter with our supernatural God? What could you do to improve your small-group meeting?

3. Give two reasons you think it is important for provision to be made for children and youth during worship services.

4. Why would it be important to give evangelism top priority in worship services? How do you think excellence in song and music affects evangelism in a worship service?

5. Have you considered tithing and financial giving to be part of your worship and ministry to God?

6. What impact could the modeling of prayer by layleaders in worship services have on the congregation?

7. How often do you pray for others? Do you see a need to increase this?

8. Have you ever participated in concert prayer? Read Acts 4:1–3,23–24. Share your needs or concerns with your small group and have a time of concert prayer.

Appendix 1:
The Later Years

The new sanctuary on Yoido Island was ready just in time to host the tenth World Pentecostal Conference. On September 23, 1973, the last day of the conference, people packed into the 10,000-seat auditorium for the dedication service. Included were five thousand conference participants from thirty-six countries.

Just before the conference, Jashil Choi founded the church's prayer and fasting retreat—Prayer Mountain—an hour's drive from Yoido in hilly country near the church cemetery.

By this time Dr. Cho knew that God wanted more than just the largest church in Korea. God was calling the church to a worldwide vision, to become missions partners with God. Dr. Cho often said, "Our church accepts the biblical mandate to take the gospel into all the world. No power on earth can deter the mighty advance of the church when the Holy Spirit is permitted to equip and empower His people for evangelism. For it is 'Not by might nor by power, but by my Spirit, says the Lord Almighty'" (Zechariah 4:6).

The church sent its first foreign missionary, Sooyoung Park, to build a church among Korean nationals living in France. YFGC held its first Annual Missions Convention in May 1974, complete with the pageantry of flags from around the world and firsthand testimonies of God's work and power in other lands. Each year afterward, YFGC appointed and sent more missionaries.

The cell group system also continued to expand, and by November 1974, there were 542 home cells serving the membership of well over sixteen thousand. By 1976—eighteen years after the church had begun under a tent—the church reported almost thirty-six thousand members and more than 1600 cell groups. The need for more office space and classrooms prompted construction on the twelve-story education building.

Developing and Strengthening Ministries

The late Dr. Donald McGavran, known as the father of church growth, visited the congregation during this time. He said it was "the best organized church in the world" and suggested that Dr. Cho begin a program to encourage and teach the many visiting pastors. After all, what God teaches us we are to share with others.

Dr. Cho had reluctantly released Dad to head the Assemblies of God mission in Vietnam in 1970, and later sent a Korean missionary to help him. Saigon fell in 1975, and Dr. Cho invited Dad and Mom to return and establish a ministry to train visiting pastors. I joined them on staff, and the renewed partnership gave birth to Church Growth International in November 1976.

We hosted the church's first international pastors' seminar in June 1977, with 577 participants, including 210 American church leaders and 119 Thai church leaders. I will never forget the electric sense of excitement as 2,100 pastors and other church leaders attended the first overseas seminar, held in Bangkok, Thailand. Soon we formed an advisory board and added other pastors from various countries as the program grew.

In 1978, Church Growth International produced a quarterly English magazine, first known as *World of Faith* and later called *Church Growth.* The importance of the printed word continued, and in October 1978, the church expanded the weekly *Full Gospel News,* and soon members used the four-page newspaper as an evangelistic tool.

As the congregation at YFGC grew, so did the need for adult Christian education. In December 1978, the church founded the Institute for Full Gospel Education (later named Youngsan Institute and is now the Education Division) for the purpose of developing written materials to teach Bible and theology to laypeople. One of its first projects was to write a seven-year curriculum for the cell groups, based on more than four hundred of Dr. Cho's past sermons.

As other needs grew, the church developed new ministries to meet those needs. Businessmen rallied to form the church's Full Gospel Businessmen's Fellowship Union. In August 1979, the Union started hosting monthly dinner meetings to reach other businessmen with the gospel. They also raised support to expand Dr. Cho's television program into Japan.

On November 4, 1979—twenty-one years after it began—the church celebrated a membership of one-hundred thousand. Pat Robertson, founder and host of the *700 Club,* spoke at the celebration worship service. The church continued to strengthen existing ministries, and seven thousand home groups were now vital to the fabric of the church. Even more foreign pastors came to see the church, now considered a divine phenomenon.

On November 30, 1981, the church celebrated a membership of two-hundred thousand including more than fourteen thousand home cell groups. In just two years, church membership had doubled. The guest speaker for this celebration event was Demos Shakarian, founder of Full Gospel Businessmen's Fellowship International.

By that time Church Growth International had held a hundred seminars for forty thousand foreign pastors and church leaders. When Dad and our family returned to America in November 1981, Dr. Ilsuk Cha, former vice-mayor of Seoul and now an elder in the church, became coordinator of this ministry.

The church's missions outreach continued to grow. Missions associations functioned in Europe, America, and Japan. Seminaries to train Korean pastors were begun in Berlin, New York, Chicago, Los Angeles, and Kobe, Japan. Church Growth International expanded into television, and soon Dr. Cho's weekly television programs aired on select stations in America. A new thirteen-story building sprang up to accommodate the World Mission Center (its vacated facility becoming the education building), and Korean missionaries served in more than ten countries. No longer was growth itself of singular importance; members felt God was calling them to excel in each of their endeavors.

Making a Difference in Society

By the 1980s, South Korea had changed. The national economy had vastly improved, and many people were now more prosperous. Foreign visitors enjoyed Seoul's luxurious hotels and modern roadways. Former American military men marveled at the strides the country had made since the war.

However, there still were problems. There was still a large number of less fortunate people. A few segments of society, as diverse as police officers and university professors, remained largely untouched by the church.

In 1982, Dr. Cho began the Practice Love Movement, whose activities of practical help continue to this day. The Women's Fellowship collects a "rice tithe" from home cell leaders and each Sunday receives donations of used clothing. In 1986 alone the women distributed 275 tons of rice to the poor and needy. From 1982 to 1987, the church gave 320,000 clothing items to 1,020 orphanages, shelters for the elderly, and the indigent of villages and islands. Since 1984, it has given nearly $1.5 million for heart surgeries for eight hundred poor, young people.

While the church continued to link people in the expanding cell groups, businessmen and church elders developed outreach fellowships to target specific groups: military personnel, university professors, police officers, prison inmates, professional athletes, and people who were blind and disabled.

As growth spiraled, the main sanctuary was renovated and enlarged in 1982, with plans to accommodate thirty-five thousand at one time. In 1983, the church was in its twenty-fifth year and reported more than three hundred thirty thousand members—having averaged a growth rate of eleven thousand members a year. By that time Prayer Mountain was receiving an average of fifteen hundred visitors a day and had built a ten-thousand-seat auditorium at the prayer and fasting retreat. Each church ministry and department expanded, with new outreaches being added to adapt to changing needs.

The year 1984 marked a special anniversary—the 100th anniversary of Protestant Christianity in Korea; on this occasion the church was renamed Yoido Full Gospel Church (YFGC). Billy Graham preached in one of the seven Sunday services. He later said, "I felt the presence of the Holy Spirit permeate the main sanctuary. My words flowed freely when I spoke."

On October 1, 1984, church membership topped four hundred thousand. At the same time, interdenominational demand for Dr. Cho was increasing: He spoke at events like Billy Graham's Itinerant Evangelists' Conference in Amsterdam and the National Religious Broadcasters Convention in Washington, D.C. By the end of 1985, Dr. Cho left 342 pastoral staff and nearly 200 administrative staff in charge whenever he went on his trips.

Jashil Choi, Dr. Cho's coworker throughout the years, retired in October 1985 to spend her time in ministry in Korean churches abroad. The overseas work continued to grow. The church had sent 261 Korean missionaries to twenty-seven countries by October 1988. The work was also progressing nationally. Agape Line, a counseling telephone ministry to Seoul residents run by laypeople, began in 1980. Dr. Cho began a ten-minute "dial-a-sermon" in 1986, logging one million calls by June 1988.

Membership had climbed to 510,000 by the end of 1986. By then the church had made the transition to computerized record keeping. In 1988, membership leapt to 600,000. Throughout this time, the layleadership base of the church continually expanded. In 1988 alone, the church appointed ten thousand new layleaders. During that year the church also completed the multimillion-dollar Elim Welfare Town, the largest facility in Asia for housing the homeless elderly and for training disadvantaged youth in marketable skills.

YFGC established branch churches, called regional sanctuaries, around the sprawling city of Seoul during the 1980s. By 1992, twelve regional sanctuaries welcomed up to twenty-two thousand people to their Sunday services.

The church continued holding annual church growth seminars for foreign pastors, featuring speakers like C. Peter Wagner, Robert Schuller, and Pat Robertson. By 1990, Church Growth International reported a combined total of more than one million participants from forty countries in its seminars and in Dr. Cho's overseas speaking engagements.

YFGC reported a membership of 645,296 in January 1992, representing 324,550 families, ministered to by 478 elders, 63,822 deacons and deaconesses, and a full-time pastoral staff of 705. At that point the church had sent 353 missionaries to 267 churches in 32 countries.

What is in store for the future? No one but the Lord knows. One thing seems certain: The members of this church have learned the power of partnership with God and with each other. It is a pattern of power that can be applied anywhere, by anyone who dares to enter a similar partnership with God.

ANNUAL GROWTH OF MEMBERSHIP*

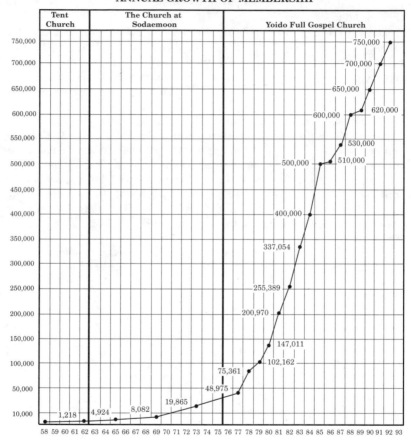

*Began to expand with more independent churches (1992–1993)

Appendix 2: Deacons in One Church in America

One church in America with a similar approach to deacons and deaconesses is First Assembly of God in Phoenix, pastored by Dr. Tommy Barnett. In 1992 it had a weekly attendance of twelve thousand, noted in *Time* magazine as the sixth largest church in America.[1]

By November 1991, Phoenix First Assembly had three kinds of deacons: administrative deacons, who serve on the official church board; ministry deacons, who oversee one of that church's more than 140 ministries; and visitation deacons and deaconesses, who weekly visit their area's church families, first-time visitors, and new converts.

Aided with information coordinated by a sophisticated computer software program, in their first two weeks nearly three hundred visitation deacons and deaconesses had visited twelve hundred homes; by the end of three months that total had climbed to ten thousand homes. These deacons and deaconesses also do altar work, dispense communion, pray for the sick, and respond to crisis situations. Weekly reports show that this activity has resulted in numerous salvations, healings, and spiritual growth.

One woman with a cystic tumor in her breast told of a visit from her deaconess, who prayed for her healing. That same day she was due to be tested by her doctor. The doctor reported that he could no longer find a trace of the tumor and canceled her surgery.

According to Staff Pastor Leo Godzich, their deacons' program has also resulted in a caring network of communication. An example of this occurred one Monday morning when Godzich received a telephone call that a drunk driver had killed a thirty-seven-year-old woman in their church. The accident critically injured her husband and son, who were air-evacuated to separate hospitals.

Before Godzich left for the hospital, he accessed the name of that family's deacon on computer and called him. By the time Godzich arrived at the husband's hospital, his deacon, Clarence Huntley, was already at his bedside praying for him. At that same time Susan Huntley, a deaconess, was praying with the son at the other hospital.

Senior Pastor Barnett arrived to pray with them an hour and a half later. The deacons contacted the Women's Ministry, who helped prepare food for the family and the funeral. All that week, though he had lost his wife, the man kept remarking to visiting friends and neighbors, "You wouldn't believe our church and how they have cared."

Even during the funeral the family's relatives remarked how much the church cared. The local news media covered the funeral and put a fifty-second spot of the preaching in its Saturday coverage. At the funeral itself, attended by several hundred, 110 people received Jesus Christ as their personal Lord and Savior.

Appendix 3: Three Kinds of Group Systems

Church growth experts C. Peter Wagner and Win Arn recommend small groups as practical channels for the local church to increase and retain its growth.[1] Many local churches now include small-group programs among their ministries. The focus of these small groups ranges from Bible study to prayer, from task to fellowship, and from social concern to outreach and evangelism. Some focus on a combination of these elements.

But a question still remains: If the world's largest church has a vast network of home groups, why is it that every church with small groups does not grow?

After I had served on YFGC's staff for five years, I returned to America eager to share with pastors and congregations what I had learned. For the next seven years I spoke, consulted, and observed churches throughout the United States. Some churches with small groups had significant growth, but many did not. I realized that just as there are several factors—human and divine—that result in the growth of an entire church, so also are there factors that result in a group system that brings dynamic spiritual life and growth. The most important factor is the kind of support system that undergirds those groups. I discovered three types of support systems, each with different results. I call them the Appendage System, the Incorporated System, and the Integrated System.

The Appendage System

One type of small group program is the Appendage System, present in 10 to 20 percent of churches with small groups. This system is begun by a layperson who has a desire to see groups developed in the congregation. The role of the senior pastor is to give permission to a layperson to start groups and to make announcements about the groups during worship services or place occasional invitations in the bulletin. This is the easiest of the three systems to build, for it is initiated and run by laypeople, with the senior pastor and pastoral staff playing only occasional supportive roles.

The same layperson who starts the Appendage System typically serves as the coordinator. He or she usually selects group leaders from among church friends and acquaintances, giving sporadic leadership training.[2] Because this laycoordinator has limited time and experience, he manages the groups through informal means, occasionally calling on the telephone or meeting group leaders in the church foyer after a worship service. He might have infrequent meetings with the senior pastor, but beyond the pastor's brief word of commendation or concern, little evaluation is done.

Group leaders determine what will be studied or discussed.[3] Most groups in an Appendage System tend to be either study groups, where participants desire more knowledge of the Bible, or fellowship groups, where participants seek to grow in Christ-centered relationships.

The response to an Appendage System is limited, usually embracing less than 20 percent of the congregation. This is largely because the vision for the groups does not come from the church's primary leadership.[4] The congregation therefore sees the groups as an "appendage" to more important church activities.

Those involved in the groups benefit from the Bible study and relationship building that occurs. Many will tell you they grew more spiritually when in those groups than at any other time of their lives. But if the laycoordinator resigns or leaves, the entire system quickly dissolves. Because the laycoordinator is the primary "vision carrier" for the groups, that person's absence creates a loss of that vision.

The Incorporated System

The Incorporated System is the most common of the three types of systems and is present in an estimated 80 to 90 percent of churches with small groups. In this system, the senior pastor begins with a desire to have groups in his church. He then delegates development and oversight of those proposed groups to a single person or committee, usually a staff pastor.[5] The senior pastor then promotes the groups to church leadership and the congregation.

Typically, the staff coordinator selects group leaders among the church's pool of existing layleaders. Often in larger churches the senior pastor also makes a general invitation to the congregation, with volunteers going through an initial leadership training. Once the groups start, the staff coordinator looks within the groups for additional leaders. Ongoing training often consists of monthly leaders' meetings.

Evaluation of the staff coordinator in an Incorporated System is based on the performance of the groups he oversees. Often the staff coordinator submits a weekly or monthly report to the senior pastor, showing the number of current groups and the number of people who attended those group meetings.

This group coordinator ideally is a full-time pastoral staff member who focuses solely on the development of that group system. However, in most churches, the groups are just one portion of that staff member's responsibilities. Smaller churches may have a designated laycoordinator. Because the coordinator's time is limited, his management tends to be administrative rather than developmental.

There are two management styles in the Incorporated System. In the "single cell management" style the coordinator relates directly to all the group leaders. In the "middle management" style, experienced layleaders are developed to oversee group leaders (similar to YFGC's section layleaders). In this style, the staff coordinator oversees several couples or individuals, who in turn oversee other group leaders.

Many churches with Incorporated Systems have all the groups study the same curriculum, whether it is published or developed by that church. Some churches even have the groups discuss the pastor's previous Sunday sermon, an acceptable practice as long as group participants attended church that Sunday. In a growing trend, other churches encourage a variety of groups, allowing each group to choose its own curriculum.

Response to an Incorporated System ranges from 20 to 50 percent of the congregation.[6] Although the senior pastor considers the groups important, the congregation sees them as another program incorporated into the many activities of the church. The Incorporated System therefore has moderate to significant impact in a church. It is one of the best ways to develop a network of pastoral care in a congregation. It is also a solid avenue of assimilation for new members.

The Integrated System

In the third system, participation in groups is recognized as essential to the life of the church. Groups are more than another program; they are an aspect of a member's churchgoing life-style. If you were to ask someone in an Integrated System to describe his weekly church schedule, he would probably say, "Well, I attend my church's worship service once a week, and I go to my home group."

While Integrated Systems are present in fewer than 1 percent of churches with small groups, they bring the greatest congregational response—often 80 to 90 percent of these congregations become involved in their church's small groups. The churches with the Integrated System—as at YFGC—are the ones that continue to grow.

The senior pastor is the key to an Integrated System. He initiates and births the groups and continues to clearly communicate the vision of small groups to his leaders and congregation. He has a multiple pastoral and laystaff to oversee the groups, but his role does not end there; he is also a ministry model to his staff, frequently meeting and ministering to them.

This multiple staff is perhaps the most outstanding distinctive of an Integrated System. Up to 80 percent of the pastoral staff are involved in its oversight. Because of this, it is not unusual to have up to 80 percent of the church's layleadership involved in group ministry.

There are two basic models of the Integrated System. In the "adapted model" the church allows some traditional patterns or programs to coexist. However, the best impact and results come in the "refined model," when an ideal 80 percent of full-time pastoral staff focus solely on personal ministry to group leaders and participants and on leadership development—of both group leaders and "middle management." Staff ministry in this model is more aggressive, focusing on home and business ministry visits.

The elements of leadership selection and staff training help select and educate potential leaders from among group assistants, observing and encouraging them at every point possible. While initial leadership training might have a lecture format, staff pastors primarily use a practical approach in ongoing leadership development: Staff members and middle management often visit group leaders in their homes and businesses and encourage leaders to accompany them to ministry events. Since full-time pastoral staff members initiate and model pastoral care, group leaders and groups are freer to be more involved in evangelism.

Typically, groups in an Integrated System study the same curriculum, written and developed by that church.[7] This curriculum is user friendly, with relevant subjects that illustrate practical biblical principles.

This system usually has mixed-purpose groups, often with a high value placed on worship, thus leading some to call them house churches. Some pastors fear that such groups will split off from the mother church; however, due to close supervision of and relationship with pastoral staff it is rare that these groups leave the local church.

Unlike an Incorporated System, an Integrated System does not develop quickly. Its primary challenge is that it requires time to develop fully. However, there are immediate benefits, and the church is

THREE KINDS OF GROUP SYSTEMS			
ASPECT	**THE APPENDAGE SYSTEM**	**THE INCORPORATED SYSTEM**	**THE INTEGRATED SYSTEM**
Role of the Senior Pastor	Permission-giver with limited support	Delegator who promotes groups to congregation	Initiator, vision bearer, and ministry model
Group Coordinator(s)	Layperson with limited time	Single staff pastor who primarily administrates	Multiple staff involved in ongoing personal ministry and "hands-on" training
Basis of Staff Evaluation	Since "staff" is lay-coordinator, no consistent evaluation is done	Based on the performance of the groups as a "program," with focus on number of groups and number of those attending group meetings	1. Frequency and impact of personal ministry to leaders and others 2. Effectiveness of lay-leaders they help choose and train (Did leaders evangelize?)
Management Style	Informal, basically to give needed information	Administrative and does some leadership training 1. "Single cell." Best with less than 12 groups 2. "Middle management." Best with continual flow of training and motivation	Oriented to personal ministry and "hands-on" training. 1. Adapted model, allowing some traditional patterns of programs to coexist 2. Refined model, with staff's main focus on personal ministry and leadership development
Leadership Selection and Training	Selects friends and acquaintances; gives sporadic training	Usually selects from volunteers or from pool of church's existing lay-leaders; often initial 4–20 hours training is by lecture, with ongoing monthly meetings	Encourages and chooses potential leaders from assistants; initial training often lecture, with frequent "hands-on" and high amount of staff interaction
Curricula	Usually chosen and/or developed by each group leader	Either all groups study same curriculum, or diversity allowed according to group type	All groups study the same curriculum developed by the church
Most Common Kind of Group	Bible study or fellowship group	Fellowship group, unless a variety of groups are encouraged	Mixed purpose groups, often high value placed on worship, in some cases a "house church"
Response of Congregation	10–20% involved; see groups as an "appendage"	20–50% involved; sees groups as optional, "incorporated" with other church programs	80–90% involved; sees group participation as "integrated" into a member's regular life-style
Impact	Limited. But for those involved, Bible study and relationship-building take place	Moderate to significant impact on congregation; good network of pastoral care and avenue for assimilation	Highly significant impact on congregation; only system that results in widespread evangelism
Potential Problems	1. "Maintenance" thinking in the minds of the group leaders ("Let's just keep what we have.") 2. Departure of the lay-coordinator	1. Reduced promotion by the senior pastor 2. Inadequate leadership training 3. Overinvolved leaders 4. Dull curriculum 5. Overloaded coordinator 6. "Two year plateau"	Some potential problems in this system can be similar to that in others; but the most frequent is discouragement, for this system takes years to develop, requiring staff to shift from a focus on programs to a focus on personal ministry and leadership development

strengthened in the process. It took twelve years from the time groups began at YFGC until they reached a ratio of one group for every twenty members in the congregation; yet even during this period YFGC grew from three thousand to more than twenty thousand.

One example of an adapted model of an Integrated System in the United States is Victory Assembly in Metairie, Louisiana, pastored by Frank Bailey. Victory has had cell groups since its start in 1979. That church now welcomes twenty-five hundred to its Sunday morning worship service. Over seventeen hundred also participate in 150 weekly cell groups, overseen by five full-time pastoral staff members who spend half their days in personal ministry with group leaders and group members. According to Parris Bailey, a staff pastor and wife of the senior pastor, Victory Assembly's cell groups surged with excitement and growth when they started to focus on the needy—the homeless and the poor living in government projects—in the surrounding New Orleans area. Outreach cell groups hold rallies in these government projects, resulting in hundreds of decisions for Jesus Christ.

Victory Assembly has four types of groups: women's groups, family groups, singles' groups, and combined youth and children's groups. Eighty of their cells are for women, some meeting in the daytime and others in the evening. The women's groups began one year after the church started in 1979. Some women's groups are outreach groups, going to prisons, orphanages, and nursing homes. A few are "helps" groups, helping with cooking, cleaning, and making banners for the church. Most groups meet for Bible study, prayer, ministry, and fellowship. They focus their evangelism on women they are acquainted with.

Another example of an adapted Integrated System is New Hope Community, pastored by Dale Galloway, in Portland, Oregon. New Hope began in 1972 with fifty people who met at an outdoor drive-in theater. Twenty years later, New Hope had fifty-eight hundred in its Sunday morning services and sixty-one hundred in its 525 small groups, called TLC (Tender Loving Care) Groups. Group leaders are called laypastors, and they are overseen by a multiple staff of four pastors, each responsible for a geographical district, and more than twenty staff pastors over specialty districts, including such areas as children, singles, seniors, youth, and support groups.

The leading example of an Integrated System in the Philippines is Cathedral of Praise in Manila, pastored since 1980 by Dr. David Sumrall. All ministry functions in that 17,000-member church are channeled through its integrated cell system. In addition to weekly adult cell groups that meet in homes, they also have children's cell groups and college cell groups, the latter meeting on campuses. Each of their four choirs and thirteen fellowships are divided into cell groups.

Even their pastoral staff meets weekly in special cell groups for prayer and Bible study; board members meet in monthly cell groups. Their nearly one thousand groups are overseen by a pastoral staff of fifty-one and more than one hundred section layleaders, who spend a great portion of their time in home visitation of group participants and church members.[8]

Still, the foremost example of an Integrated System is Korea's YFGC, which first started with groups in 1964. Now more than 80 percent of its nearly eight hundred pastoral staff and the majority of its nearly seventy thousand layleaders are involved with the groups and their participants. The staff pastors' daily job descriptions involve scheduled ministry visits to the homes of members and layleaders.

Even though it takes time and consistent work to develop the pastoral staff and ministry dynamic in an Integrated System, it is well worth the effort. Only in the Integrated System is there maximum congregational involvement, and only in such a system does evangelism increase systemwide, with groups that make a positive difference.

Appendix 4:
Home Visitation in
Church History

Pastoral ministry visits used to be a vital part of church life in Europe and America. Richard Baxter, born in England in 1615, has been called "the most outstanding pastor, evangelist, and writer on practical and devotional themes that Puritanism produced."[1] Baxter was the vicar of Kidderminster, an English town with eight hundred homes and two thousand people. His practice was to preach on Sunday, then visit fifteen to sixteen families in their homes on Monday and Tuesday. He called his home ministry "private catechism."

He later wrote a treatise for young preachers called *The Reformed Pastor*. In it he said that this private catechism benefited some people more than "ten years of public preaching." He said, "If we had but set about this business sooner, who knows how many souls might have been brought to Christ, and how much happier our congregations might have been?"[2]

Baxter further suggested that when the number grew in the congregation, pastors should add one or two assistants to help them in visitation and not "content themselves with public preaching, as if that were all that was necessary."[3]

George Whitefield, considered the most outstanding evangelist of the 1700s, visited Kidderminster seventy-two years after Baxter left. Whitefield wrote about the long-lasting results of Baxter's ministry, remarking that it greatly refreshed him to see the "sweet savor" remaining from Baxter's fourteen years of "doctrine, works, and discipline."[4]

In the 1800s, the "prince of preachers" was Charles Spurgeon. He made a consistent practice of having his wife read Baxter's book, *The Reformed Pastor*, to him every Sunday after he finished preaching.[5]

Another who benefited from Baxter's example was John Wesley, founder of Methodism, who read *The Reformed Pastor* and told his circuit preachers to go from house to house.[6] One itinerant preacher of John Wesley's day reported stopping at each home along the way to say he had come to talk about religion. Another stated that he spent the first two weeks at a location, visiting house to house, getting to know the people.[7]

Home Visitation in Recent Times

Pastoral visitation was frequent in the West until the 1950s. Perry Gresham, in those days president of Bethany College in Bethany, West Virginia, wrote, "The inclination to look upon visitation as unworthy of a preacher's time is an attitude of pride approaching arrogance. The first churches were the homes of members who opened their doors to their fellow Christians. The apostles brought blessing to those houses and received a blessing in return . . . No man can preach adequately unless he visits the homes of his people when they need him. More often than not, he receives a greater blessing than he leaves."[8]

E. S. Williams, general superintendent of the Assemblies of God from 1929 to 1949—the same denomination Dr. Yonggi Cho belongs to—wrote, "In pastoral visitation the pastor comes nearer his people than any other way, learning of their struggles, needs, disappointments, and learning to appreciate them with a compassionate love that he otherwise could not know."[9]

Ralph Riggs, general superintendent of the Assemblies of God from 1953 to 1956, ranked pastoral visitation equal in importance to preaching and saw the two linked together: "Apart from the Bible and one's own prayer life, there is no better sermon material than pastoral visitation. As home after home is visited and discovery is made of the spiritual state of people, . . . the pastor . . . can now talk about the very thing that they want to hear and need to know . . . Such sermons as these really build and help the people."[10]

One pastor's diary, published in 1937, is filled with accounts of home visitation. He wrote, "I should not think of belittling public teaching, but in my work it seems to me more is accomplished by teaching them from house to house as Paul speaks of doing."[11]

Why don't we see this emphasis today? What happened to this practice that helped fuel revival fires of the past? Two things weakened it. First, pastors usually didn't take laymen with them on these visits. As congregations grew larger and larger, one pastor visiting every home became an overwhelming task. Also, in later times these visits contained less ministry; they became mere social calls.

Was it any wonder that pastors felt they could make better use of their time? Visitation was relegated to older staff pastors who made hospital calls or to a small core of layleaders who followed up first-time visitors.

One other thing nearly halted pastoral visitation altogether. By the 1960s, churches began modeling themselves after secular businesses by hiring multiple staff specialists, such as ministers of visitation, ministers of youth, ministers of music, and ministers of education. While there was legitimate need for certain specialty areas, like music, most churches reduced pastoral care to one program, or a series, that they would administrate. Rather than home visitation being everyone's job—pastor and church members—it became the job of the hired staff specialist or a handful of laymen.

Examples of Churches with Layministry Visitation

In addition to evangelistic teams that follow up on first time visitors, a few American churches have organized teams of people, under one or more staff pastors, to make home ministry visits to church members.

Love Center Christian Fellowship in Tulsa, Oklahoma, reported visiting every church family, whether the family were formal members, visitors, or simply attended services. Soon afterward, the church office reported a surge in church membership. Senior Pastor William Gardner wrote that since being involved in visitation, his church has been having "more visitors, an increase in financial giving, and a greater commitment to the ministries of the church . . . The personal touch present in home visitation produces closer relationships among those in our church. Many have experienced a healing in this process."[12]

For three months, Upper Room Assembly of God in Miami, Florida, had visitation teams that visited 190 homes of church families. Several answers to prayer were reported, ranging from employment to physical healings to salvations. Staff Pastor Bill Adkins wrote, "The Sunday morning attendance has grown. There has also been a growing amount of bonding going on in the congregation. We see now how cell groups are birthed out of visitation."[13] Upper Room has now incorporated visitation into their fifty home groups.

Examples of Churches with Pastoral Visitation

Churches that benefit the most are those with multiple pastoral staff directly involved in ministry visitation. Presently only one church in America—8,500-member Victory Outreach Center of Tulsa, Oklahoma—reports a multiple pastoral staff that focus on home ministry visits. This staff of eleven "care pastors" discovered that because both husbands and wives often work, most ministry visits need to be made in the evening. Most care pastors officially start their working days at noon and do not conclude until 8:00 P.M., also visiting all day Saturday. Each care pastor is responsible to visit between 300 and 350 families during the course of a year.[14]

Another church in Asia with a strong focus on pastoral visitation is Cathedral of Praise in Manila, Philippines. Persons applying for membership in Cathedral of Praise are asked to indicate the two or three times each week they are most likely to be home. Each member is visited in his home once every ninety days by his area pastor and once every thirty days by his cell group leader.

When Dr. David Sumrall began to pastor Cathedral of Praise in 1980, there were eight hundred in the congregation. Sumrall initiated a strong focus on visitation in 1984, and by 1994 Cathedral of Praise had grown to a membership of seventeen thousand with nearly one thousand cell groups. Each person on its 51-member pastoral staff now visits thirty to thirty-five homes every week, with twenty pastoral interns each required to make fifty weekly new-convert follow-up visits.

Visits are unannounced, allowing an area pastor to observe and minister to a family in its most natural setting. In visitation and other activities, pastoral staff members and layleaders follow a practice termed "shadowing." Layleaders are encouraged to accompany, or "shadow," a staff pastor and thereby observe and learn from him. It is a practical training that more fully equips the layleader.

Dr. Sumrall reports, "There are two main benefits from pastoral visitation. First, many in a new Christian's family are not born again. Visiting a new convert in his home gives us an opportunity to share the gospel with others in the family. We have seen many come to the Lord this way, bringing more growth to our church. Secondly, visiting a member's home allows us to show him that we really care for him as a person. He knows then that our love for him is more than rhetoric; it is a reality. Through home visitation and cell groups we have closed the back door of our church."[15]

Endnotes

Introduction

[1]Dr. John Vaughan is assistant professor of Church Growth at Southwest Baptist University in Bolivar, Missouri. He is the author of several church growth books, including *Megachurches and America's Cities* (Grand Rapids: Baker Books, 1993). The Korean church closest in size to YFGC is in NamBu with 105,000 members, pastored by Yonggi Cho's younger brother, Yongmok Cho. He applies many of the same principles and practices found in his older brother's church.

[2]The three years of the Korean War (1950–1953) were preceded by thirty-five years of Japanese occupation (1910–1945).

[3]Mark Hoffman, ed., *The World Almanac and Book of Facts: 1992* (New York: Pharos Books, 1991), 953.

[4]United States Bureau of the Census. Statistical Abstract of the United States: 1989 (Washington, D.C.: U.S. Government Printing Office, 1989), 172 (charts 290 and 291).

[5]William Dudley, ed., *Poverty* (St. Paul: Greenhaven Press, 1988), 18.

[6]Hoffman, World Almanac, 951.

[7]John Wauck, "Paganism American Style," *National Review*, 19 March 1990, 43–44.

[8]I was grateful that Lee Weeder accompanied me on my 1989 research trip, for she helped me do research on YFGC. She was an able interpreter and translator in interviews and testimonies, and I remain appreciative for her help, prayer, and insights. I am also thankful for her husband, Gil Weeder, for allowing us to go on that trip, and for Stan Telchin, her supportive pastor.

Chapter 1: The Early Years

[1]Burton Stevenson, ed., *The Home Book of Quotations,* 10th ed. (New York: Dodd, Mead and Company, 1976), 146. This proverb is quoted by Aristotle in *Politics*, book 5, chap. 3, sec. 30.

[2]Ralph Bird was the founding pastor of Faith Memorial Church in Atlanta, Georgia. Dad and Ralph Bird had also ministered together in Liberia and seen thousands saved, filled with the Spirit, and healed. This was the pilot project of Global Conquest, an evangelistic campaign ministry of the Assemblies of God Division of Foreign Missions. Today such campaigns are called Good News Crusades.

[3]The Korean Assemblies of God believes that healing is vital to God's plan for our day. However, because there were so few qualified professors and guest lecturers then in the Korean Assemblies of God, guest speakers from other denominations were invited. Some who did not believe in divine healing taught the students their beliefs. This gave rise to the confusion that Cho and others were to struggle with.

[4]This effort was coordinated through Maynard Ketcham, then Far East field secretary of the Division of Foreign Missions of the Assemblies of God, and J. Philip Hogan, executive director. The speaker of the tent crusade at the beginning of the Sodaemoon church was Evangelist Sam Todd.

[5]Missionary John Stetz helped in acquisition of the Sodaemoon property. He became pastor of those who remained with the church in Bulkwangdong. That church continues today.

[6]When Yonggi Cho first began the tent church, he was in the Korean Assemblies of God. However, because some then disagreed with his stand on healing and prosperity, he left the Korean Assemblies, and the tent church became an independent work. Dad worked to get him back into the Assemblies. The church has continued in the Korean Assemblies of God, except for a brief period in the early 1980s.

[7]Missionaries Henry and Lydia Swain went to help Yonggi Cho during this time. After her husband's death, Lydia returned to work as Cho's personal secretary and continues in that position at the time of this writing. Other missionaries who helped Dr. Cho in later years include John and Edith Stetz, Art and Ruth Sholtis, Bob and Naomi Malone, and Jennie Teske. Warner Miles later worked with Dr. Cho in establishing other churches. Ruth Sholtis served as managing editor of the English quarterly *Church Growth* from 1982 to 1989. These were Assemblies of God missionaries under the Division of Foreign Missions, J. Philip Hogan, executive director. Jack Holm, an independent Pentecostal missionary, also worked with Dr. Cho.

[8]The old Sodaemoon site later became the headquarters building of the Korean Assemblies of God, as well as a local church for those who remained behind.

Chapter 2: The Ministry of Prayer

[1]At the time of this writing, Changpyo Yim, formerly a YFGC staff pastor, is staff pastor of a Korean church in America.

[2]According to Korean church history, Presbyterian Pastor Sunjoo Kil and his friend Chirok Pak initiated early morning prayer when they invited others to join them in their prayer time of waiting on God. For further details see Colin Whittaker, *Korean Miracle* (Eastborne, England: Kingsway Publications, 1988), 59–61.

[3]Three stated times of prayer for later Judaism were at nine in the morning, three in the afternoon, and sunset. Since each early morning prayer meeting in Korea has preaching or teaching as a segment, it is felt that this is a biblical pattern.

[4]South Koreans typically work five and a half days a week, including half a day of work on Saturday. Some work six days a week.

[5]In my random survey of 425 cell leaders, a little more than half (52.7 percent) indicated that they regularly attend one all-night prayer meeting each week. Cell leaders with groups of nine or more were statistically more frequent in their participation in all-night prayer meetings than were cell leaders with groups of eight or fewer.

[6]This is reflected in Jesus' words to Paul in Acts 26:17–18; Paul's letter to the Ephesians in Ephesians 1:19–23; 2:2; 6:12; Paul's letter to the Corinthians in 2 Corinthians 10:3–4; Hebrews 1:3–4; and Peter's letter in 1 Peter 5:8.

[7]Edward E. Plowman, ed., "The New Evangelism," *A National and International Religion Report* (Springfield, Va.: n.p.), 1.

Chapter 3: International Prayer Mountain

[1]"YFGC International Fasting Prayer Mountain" (Seoul, Korea: YFGC Office of Public Information, n.d.).

[2]Jashil Choi, interview by author, 1979.

[3]"YFGC International Fasting Prayer Mountain."

Chapter 4: The Ministry of Layleaders

[1]In 1978, when the church kept detailed statistics on the ways people came to membership at YFGC, 75 percent came because of the influence of family, friends, or the personal witness of another. The same was true of YFGC's layleaders.

[2]Few statistics are available from the years before the home cell groups began. One example of this ratio was in September 1976, fifteen years after the appointment of deacons and deaconesses at Sodaemoon, when the church reported 30,795 registered members and 1,987

layleaders—including 367 deacons, 1,373 deaconesses, 209 senior deacons, and 38 elders. This would be one layleader for every 15.5 members.

[3]By June 1992—nearly thirty years after the revival center had become a church—there were 3,100 senior deaconesses in a congregation of more than 650,000 members; also reported were 67,505 layleaders, including 16,788 deacons, 44,748 deaconesses, 2,324 senior deacons, and 545 elders.

[4]Only on rare occasions does YFGC strip a layleader of his title. However, in no church is any layleader perfect. If there is a problem with a layleader, the person is dealt with individually, questioned and confronted by other layleaders and perhaps even a staff pastor. Often that leader has a personal problem in need of ministry, and once that issue is dealt with, he will no longer be a problem leader. If the problem persists, he is told to go to Prayer Mountain for three days of prayer and fasting if he wants to continue in leadership. Few problems have continued after that visit. If they do, a group of the church's elders intervenes to reason and pray with him. If that person continues in known sin or rebellion, one expression in the church succinctly states, "If you can't kick the devil out of the man, then you must kick the man and the devil out."

[5]The home cell leader is required to complete classes for cell leaders. Some staff pastors require that a potential leader have at least two other people who have agreed to meet with him or her before a group is allowed to start.

[6]John and Karen Hurston, *Caught in the Web* (Anaheim, Calif.: Mountain Press, 1977), 103. This book is now out of print.

[7]Various districts adopt slightly different criteria for leadership appointment. One year a certain district had a severe shortage of leaders; there were not enough assistant leaders and few volunteers. A staff pastor said that they had tried to remedy the situation by making every person who had been a member of the church at least two years a cell leader. Seasoned section leaders carefully supervised these new leaders. "The problems of a growing church," he said, "are not always easy to solve."

[8]In the past, such leaders were "carrier teachers" who took Dr. Cho's weekly lessons and shared them with their groups. As the cell system evolved and systematic written materials were developed, this changed. By 1988, leaders no longer had a weekly training meeting at the church. Printed supplemental materials are available before and after Wednesday services, at convenient locations, as helps to the lesson for that week. Group leaders continue to need both initial and ongoing training.

[9]Topics covered in the Cell Leaders' College include, among other subjects, the responsibilities of the cell leader, home cell group growth, self-discipline and self-development, Bible lesson preparation, prayer, home visitation, the Great Commission, the threefold blessing and five-fold salvation, the work of the Holy Spirit, heresy and false doctrine, worship in theory and practice, counseling and healing, and Christian ethics in living the holy and separated life. (This material is available only in Korean.)

[10]This figure is also based on responses to the previously mentioned survey mentioned in note 5, chapter 2.

[11]To qualify as a senior deacon, one also must be born again for a minimum of seven years and have a consistent tithing record. The great majority of senior deacons are currently serving, or have served, as male section leaders.

[12]A senior deaconess must be at least 50 years old.

Deaconesses between the ages of 45 and 50 are eligible to be nominated as apprentice senior deaconesses. In recent years so many deaconesses have become eligible to be senior deaconesses that one additional stipulation was added. Now every member of the senior deaconess' family must be a born-again Christian. Her husband must be an involved YFGC member, at least attending a men's home group. It is not uncommon for a wife to be a senior deaconess, and the husband to be an elder.

[13]While a handful of elders are in key paid administrative staff positions, the majority of the over seven hundred elders (as of June 1994) volunteer their service and are divided into a total of nearly forty different task force committees. Through these committees, the elders address administrative and policy matters. The largest is the Visitation Task Force Committee, composed at one time of three hundred elders. These elders serve in helping the staff pastors with visitation; many visit three to six homes a month.

Other task force committees address topics such as foreign missions, evangelism, education, personnel, finances, public relations, social welfare, gospel literature, church growth, media, church law, and Prayer Mountain. There is even an Inspection Committee that inspects every department and ministry of the church to see that funds are spent in an appropriate manner and that ministries and ministers are functioning with integrity.

Although each task force committee makes decisions or votes on a recommendation, Dr. Cho gives final confirmation. About fifteen of the top ranking elders form an executive committee serving as an advisory group and communications channel for Dr. Cho.

[14]Tensions do sometimes arise. In the mid 1970s, Dr. Cho wanted the

church to build a hospital. Because of a lack of funds and the cost of operating a hospital, the elders strongly recommended that a hospital not be built. Later, unknown facts surfaced, and Dr. Cho thanked the elders for their restraint. (The church now gives thousands of dollars to fund heart operations for indigent children in hospitals around Korea.)

[15]Each ministry area and department has an assigned elder working in tandem with a staff pastor. This assigned elder acts as a liaison between that ministry and the Finance Task Force Committee, which later determines the proposed budget for the upcoming year.

Chapter 5: Home Cell Groups

[1]When the church began, people were baptized in the Han River, so baptisms were limited to the warm summer months. At the Sodaemoon location, there was a baptistery in the platform; even so, water baptisms are limited to warm summer months. Believers who apply for membership but have not been baptized in water are expected to be baptized during the following summer months. Currently YFGC has baptisteries in a large chapel, with lengthy baptismal times set during the months of July and August.

[2]Since Yonggi Cho was not ordained the first year the church was at Sodaemoon, my father was senior pastor. But because my father was not fluent in the Korean language, Dr. Cho and Jashil Choi did most of the preaching.

[3]Not long after the home cell groups started, a need arose to be more organized. Since YFGC places high value on home ministry visits, combined with the fact that few people own cars but must rely on public transportation, the church organized the groups in geographical districts—the most convenient organization for the purposes to be accomplished.

Adjacent to Dr. Cho's inner office is a large map of the city of Seoul. The city government has divided the sprawling metropolitan area of nearly twelve million inhabitants into geographical districts. Through the years the church has either combined or divided those districts to form their own divisions. By December 1990 the church had twenty-three districts throughout the city.

In every geographical district are nearly thirty thousand church members, cell group leaders, and section leaders—cared for by their assigned staff pastors. Each district pastoral staff, composed of junior staff pastors (called subdistrict pastors), are overseen by a head pastor (called district pastors) and have desks in the same district office in the church. These staff pastors spend their days in home visitation and during church services are available in the district offices for reporting, prayer, and counseling.

⁴These weekly reports included the names of the leader, the speaker, those in attendance, those who were born again at the meeting, and the amount of the offering. Weekly reports like these were submitted for many years and are still given in the children's groups. However, because of the growth of the number of men's and women's groups since that time, the only written report now submitted to the church is the offering amount and date of the meeting on the front of the cell offering envelope.

⁵Since a primary purpose of YFGC's groups is evangelism, their homogenous consistency helps them achieve this goal. Heterogenous groups—with people unlike one another in gender, age, background, or occupation—tend to spend so much energy maintaining harmonious relationships that energy for outreach is largely dissipated. However, when a church's primary purpose is to create a sense of Christian family or community in a fractured society, heterogenous groups are preferable, although they generally will not be as evangelistic.

⁶Not all YFGC's women's groups involve homemakers. Some women work in offices and have their cell meetings during the lunch hour or at home after work. This is a growing trend, but at this point involves no more than 5 percent of the women's groups.

⁷An English translation of the first book, *The Home Cell Group Study Guide*, is available from Word Books, Milton Keynes, England, or through the church, Yoido Post Office Box 7, Seoul 150-600, Korea. Lesson titles in the first study guide include "The Purpose of Creation," "The Temptation and the Fall," "The Original Sin and Subsequent Sin," "The Passover Lamb and the Covenant of Redemption," "The Three Offices of Jesus," "Jesus Calls His Disciples," and "Peter's Confession of Faith."

⁸First and foremost, we are to love one another (John 13:34–35; Romans 13:8; 1 Peter 1:22), walking in love "just as Christ loved us and gave himself up for us" (Ephesians 5:2). We are to forgive each other, "just as in Christ God forgave [us]" (Ephesians 4:32). We are to comfort those in trouble "with the comfort we ourselves have received from God" (2 Corinthians 1:4). We also are to be at peace with one another (Mark 9:50), stop passing judgment on one another (Romans 14:13), be kind and compassionate to one another (Ephesians 4:32), encourage one another (1 Thessalonians 5:11; Hebrews 3:13), serve one another (1 Peter 4:10), offer hospitality to one another without grumbling (1 Peter 4:9), and pray for one another (James 5:16).

Carl George, author of *Prepare Your Church for the Future,* points out that twenty-one of the fifty-nine "one another" passages in Scripture call for Christians to walk in love. (Carl George, *Prepare Your Church for the Future* [Grand Rapids: Regal Press, 1992], 131.)

⁹In October 1987, with Dr. Cho's permission, I sent surveys to more than six hundred home cell leaders, and over four hundred of them were returned completed. The survey showed that the typical leader visits three to five homes each week. Because the Wednesday weekly training sessions were ended in 1988, it became difficult to repeat this survey.

¹⁰The top three leaders who have won the most people are usually section leaders who have joined with their cell leaders to reach as many people in their combined communities as possible. In a single year, most top section leaders have won people to the Lord from a hundred different families. In 1983, one section leader and her cell leaders were instrumental in leading people from over three hundred different families to the Lord and church membership. In 1989 I watched as Dr. Cho recognized and prayed for one female section leader. She, with several cell leaders in her area, had brought over two hundred people to the Lord that previous year. I made one random sample survey of 340 cell groups from eight different districts. Those groups reported that people from 472 families had been born again and applied for church membership during that past year. However, a little more than half did not report any new people in their groups being born again and applying for church membership. The remaining groups ranged from winning one to twenty-three people to the Lord during that same time.

¹¹In one survey I did, the typical cell leader prays an hour a day. More than half the cell leaders also attend one all-night prayer meeting each week. In addition, many cell and section leaders also fast for specific unbelievers. Some even go to Prayer Mountain for extended times of prayer and fasting for specific unbelievers. Prayer is to initiate and permeate the evangelism process.

¹²*Full Gospel News* (changed to *Full Gospel Family* in 1994) began in 1978 with a weekly circulation of 10,000 copies. By 1990, the church was distributing 1.4 million copies weekly. Each week the church gives each staff pastor 2,000 copies to give to leaders.

Chapter 6: The Ministry of the Pastoral Staff

¹Today, six departments administrate the church activities of the departments of general affairs, finance, education, public relations, world missions, and pastoral care. Three of these departments are headed by appointed layleaders, the other three by appointed staff pastors. A staff of more than two hundred laypeople handle administrative matters, freeing ministers to focus on pastoral concerns. The most ministry-oriented department is the Department of Pastoral Care. This department involves 90 percent of YFGC's staff pastors and is directed by the staff pastor who serves as Dr. Cho's head assistant. This depart-

ment is responsible for the adult and youth groups, the regional sanctuaries, pastoral counseling, classes and worship services for handicapped members, and the Christ Ambassador's Mission—the organization for YFGC's university students.

2For each visit, this daily report includes the name of that person's home cell leader, the name of the person or family visited, the phone number of that person, the purpose of the visit, which layleader(s) accompanied the staff pastor on the visit, the times at the beginning and end of the visit, the minisermon title or topic with the Bible passage shared, and any type of literature given to that person or family.

3Most had been born again for sixteen to twenty years, and many had been either saved or healed through the ministry of YFGC. Three out of four staff pastors had previously served as deacons or deaconesses in YFGC, while four out of five had previously served as cell leaders. A little more than half indicated that they had also been section leaders in the church before coming on staff; this tended to be more true of the women than it did of the men. I conducted this survey with Dr. Cho's permission. A total of 202 staff pastors (a cross-section of district pastors, subdistrict pastors, and intern pastors) completed the one-page survey in October 1987. The same survey was completed by a random sample of 39 staff pastors in December 1990. Overall results were the same in both surveys. The profile of the typical staff pastor was a married female between the ages of thirty-five and forty-four, who had children. She originally decided to become a believer because of the influence of parents, family, friends, or the personal witnessing of another. She had been a Christian between sixteen and twenty years, and had been attending the church between ten and fourteen years. She had previously served as cell leader, deaconess, and section leader in the church. She had been serving on staff for the last four to five years as a licensed subdistrict pastor, and spent between one and two hours in prayer each day. During the annual Grand Home Visitation she visited over three hundred homes, averaging ten home visits per day.

4Although women in YFGC have much more freedom and encouragement to be involved in ministry than is customary in Korea, there are clear boundaries. Men occupy the top leadership roles in the church, both on pastoral staff and in layleadership. Only an ordained male minister may be appointed pastor over a large geographical district; females may serve under them as subdistrict pastors. Only men may become elders and serve on the governing board of the church. However boundaries have recently been expanded. In 1994 YFGC allowed two women to become district pastors.

5Several times Dad accompanied Dr. Cho and key layleaders in their monthly visits to the church's district offices. Once I had the opportunity to go with them. In each office we entered there was always a specially prepared flip chart. One page had that district's number of new members that month, and another page had the number of new cell groups. Those numbers were contrasted with the goals that had been set. Dr. Cho was careful to commend the pastors who had reached their goals, and often all those present would applaud them. Each month, Dr. Cho spent up to forty-five minutes in each district office, reviewing progress on that area's goals. If goals were not reached, staff pastors apologetically explained specific reasons. Dr. Cho often responded with a suggestion to strengthen their resolve or a word of encouragement, always ending the visit in a time of prayer.

[6]One question I asked of the pastoral staff on a survey was this: "Honestly, how much do you pray each day?" The response was consistently an average of an hour and a half. It was unclear in the survey whether this time included the hour of prayer at the beginning of the workday or not. If this response was combined with the hour spent in prayer at the office, it approximates the three hours each is asked to pray daily. This question was posed in the previously mentioned one-page survey given twice to segments of the pastoral staff.

[7]The typical YFGC staff pastor oversees more than fifteen section layleaders, about a hundred cell groups, and up to two thousand people.

Chapter 7: Outreach Fellowships

[1]Sunghoon Myung, "Spiritual Dimension of Church Growth as Applied to Yoido Full Gospel Church" (Ph.D. diss., Fuller Theological Seminary, School of World Missions, 1990), 83.

[2]In a growing trend, forty-nine of those churches have congregations composed of half or more from the nationality of the host country.

Chapter 8: The Church's Doctrine

[1]Since the late 1980s, this official statement of faith has been repeated in each of the church's annual brochures.

[2]Dr. Cho shared this account in the annual Church Growth International Seminar in August 1988. Thousands of similar testimonies of healing remain in the fabric of YFGC's heritage.

[3]Office of Information, "Annual Church Brochure" (Yoido Full Gospel Church, 1989/90), 4.

[4]Sunghoon Myung, "Spiritual Dimension of Church Growth as Applied to Yoido Full Gospel Church." (Ph.D. Diss., Fuller Theological Seminary, School of World Missions, 1990), 87. Myung received 440 completed surveys from members of various church departments as the basis of data from which these figures are drawn.

[5]Ibid.

[6]"Annual Church Brochure," 1987, inside cover.

Chapter 9: The Sermons

[1]*Unique Illustrations of Paul Cho* (Church Growth International, Yoido Post Office Box 7, Seoul 150-600, Korea, 1989), 3.

At different times, Dr. Cho has used the Western names Paul or David for himself. However, his Korean name is Yonggi Cho, or more properly in the Korean language order, Cho Yonggi. Cho is the family name.

[2]In later years, Dr. Cho has used the theologians and writers of YFGC's Education Division (see chapter 8) to help him do background research and find relevant illustrations.

[3]His bout with tuberculosis also hampered his pursuit of education; he never formally graduated from high school. However, he started advanced studies in both medicine and law and graduated from Full Gospel Bible College when it was a Bible training institute. He has received honorary doctorate degrees from Bethany College of the Assemblies of God in Santa Cruz, California; Southeastern Assemblies of God College in Lakeland, Florida; and California Graduate School of Theology, Fresno. All who know Dr. Cho quickly tell you that he is highly intelligent and well-read.

Chapter 10: The Worship Services

[1]The church does not have a nursery, but instead provides a separate overflow room, complete with a video screen for nursing mothers.

[2]See "Sequence of Events in Most YFGC Worship Services" on page 172.

[3]One reason for this low figure is that many in Korea live in extended families, where grandparents or aunts and uncles look after children while parents take sometimes lengthy city bus rides to church. Also, YFGC, like many churches, needs to recruit even more teachers and expand facilities. The church's Education Division develops written material for these children's Sunday school classes. They keep the format fast-paced and interesting, focusing on prayer and Bible study. Each grade level has a choir that ministers in song on appropriate occasions.

[4]Tithing accounts for a little more than 60 percent of the church income, 5 to 10 percent comes from home cell offerings, and the remainder comes from pledges and freewill offerings. The monies of the mission fellowships are separate.

[5]These offering bags are then taken to a secured room, and a number of senior deacons count the enclosed money. The money is then immediately deposited in a nearby bank. The senior deacons return empty marked envelopes to the YFGC Accounting Department, headed by a

layleader with a group of assistants. No staff pastor is involved in any of these transactions, thus freeing them from any taint of financial misdealing.

Appendix 2: Deacons in One Church in America

[1]Ostling, Richard N. "Superchurches and How They Grew," *Time*, 5 August 1991.

Appendix 3: Three Kinds of Group Systems

[1]Win Arn, *The Church Growth Ratio Book* (Monrovia, Calif: Church Growth Inc., 1990), 25–34. Dr. C. Peter Wagner has given repeated verbal support of Dr. Carl George and the Fuller Institute of Evangelism and Church Growth, as well as of Rev. Dale Galloway—both deeply involved in the use of small groups for the growth of the church.

[2]Initial training is often done directly by the laycoordinator through existing published curriculum or by attending another organization's or church's training event. Usually ongoing training involves sporadic gatherings of group leaders or additional participation at training events sponsored by other organizations or churches. One popular training event for laycoordinators and their group leaders are seminars sponsored by Serendipity, an organization founded by Lyman Coleman. In recent years Serendipity also has sponsored advanced seminars more beneficial to those in an Incorporated System.

[3]In some cases this material is self-prepared, while in others it is published curriculum or material borrowed from another church's groups.

[4]If the layperson who initiated and coordinates the groups has substantial influence and recognition in the congregation, a larger number in the congregation tend to be involved. This is also true if a cluster of influential laypersons are involved in leadership. Even then, it is rare that any church with an Appendage System—no matter how large the congregation—will have more than twenty groups.

[5]In the larger church the senior pastor delegates to a staff pastor; in the smaller church he delegates to a trusted layleader or committee.

[6]There are exceptions to this 50 percent congregational "ceiling," but they are rare.

[7]Even though the groups in an Integrated System study the same curriculum, there are differences in those groups, primarily in terms of composition. For example, there are four basic compositions to YFGC's cell groups: women's groups, men's groups, youth groups (made up of young, single adults), and children's groups. Also, some churches with an Integrated System do allow particular groups to use other curriculum.

[8]Dr. David Sumrall to author, 4 June 1992. Cathedral of Praise, formerly Manila Bethel Temple, was founded by Dr. Lester Sumrall in 1954 and started from large crusades held by Clifton Erickson and others from Voice of Healing. When Sumrall became pastor of that church in 1980, it had between eight hundred and one thousand members.

Appendix 4: Home Visitation in Church History

[1]James I. Packer, introduction to *The Reformed Pastor* by Richard Baxter (Edinburgh, Scotland: Banner of Truth Trust, first published in 1656; 1971 ed.), 11.

[2]Ibid., 200.

[3]Ibid., 155.

[4]Ibid., 12.

[5]*C. H. Spurgeon: The Early Years* (London: n.p., 1962), 417.

[6]Packer, *The Reformed Pastor*, 15.

[7]Gerald O. McCulloh, ed., *The Ministry in the Methodist Heritage* (Nashville: Board of Education of the Methodist Church, 1960), 42-43.

[8]Perry Epler Gresham (president of Bethany College in Bethany, West Virginia), *Disciplines of the High Calling* (St. Louis: The Bethany Press, 1946), 97–98.

[9]E. S. Williams, *A Faithful Minister: Heart-to-Heart Talks* (Springfield, Mo.: Gospel Publishing House, 1941), 86–87.

[10]Ralph Riggs, *The Spirit-Filled Pastor's Guide* (Springfield, Mo.: Gospel Publishing House, 1948), 243.

[11]Charles Elmo Robinson, *A Pastor's Diary* (Springfield, Mo.: Gospel Publishing House, 1937), 17, 35.

[12]Love Center Christian Fellowship now has laypastors who focus on ministry visitation. This quote was taken from my correspondence with Rev. William Gardner.

[13]The senior pastor of Upper Room Assembly of God is Rev. Bruce Klepp, who continues to do some ministry visitation himself.

[14]Victory Christian Center was founded by Pastor Billy Joe Daughtery, in Tulsa, Oklahoma. It had 8,500 members as of March 1994. The care pastors mentioned are under the Care Ministry of the church, overseen by Pastors Jerry and Lynn Popenhagen, which also involves a small-group system.

[15]Dr. David Sumrall, telephone interview by author, August 1992.